I WORKED TRACTION ENGINES

by

JACK HAMPSHIRE

Camden Miniature Steam Services

British Library Cataloguing-in-Publication-Data:
a catalogue record of this book is held by the British Library.

First Printing by J. H. Lake & Co. Ltd 1967
Second Printing 1968
Third Printing 2010

ISBN No. 978-0-9564073-3-7

Published in Great Britain by:
CAMDEN MINIATURE STEAM SERVICES
Barrow Farm, Rode, Frome, Somerset. BA11 6PS
www.camdenmin.co.uk

Camden stock one of the widest selections of fine transportation,
engineering and other books; contact them at the above address for
a copy of their latest free Booklist.

FRONT COVER: the author can just be seen in the cab of his Foden 6 ton,
three-way tipping steam wagon No. 13716 "Peg O My Heart". Horsham - 10th July 1965

PLEASE NOTE:

Due to the slightly marked original copy from which most of this book was scanned, there
are some marks on certain pages which have been 'carried-over' from the original, which
we regret we have been unable to entirely eliminate.

To my brother
CYRIL

ACKNOWLEDGEMENTS

There are many people to whom I owe great thanks for the help they have given in the fulfilment of this book. Especially to two great Cornish friends; John H. Trounson, for his contribution of the foreword, and Charles Gregory, with whose name must also be coupled that of Mr. W. Boddy, of *Motor Sport*, for their unfailing interest and moral support without which this book would never have been completed.

I owe much to my wife, to " Skipper " Phillips and Agatha Child for their tireless efforts in the revision of the text; to the surviving relatives of old employees for certain photographs, and to Gordon O. Lugg for supplying the maker's numbers of two of our engines, taken from the records kept by the late Mr. Chris Lambert, of Horsmonden.

JACK HAMPSHIRE.

Introduction

FOR MANY YEARS I had been forced to believe that the Traction Engine and the Road Locomotive were banished from our roads for ever by what some people like to refer to as progress. For those of us who lived and worked with them, they could never die. So long as we live, they will remain in our hearts.

From early childhood I learned the music of the exhaust's staccato " bark " and the ring of the gears. Even today the sound of a Traction Engine running under steam, alas, now only on the rally field, sets my heart bounding. Nostalgic memories carry me swiftly back through the years, and once again, in fantasy, I am on the footplate driving one of those " Majestic Monarchs of the Road," The long hours worked in one day, the heavy duties performed, the pittance one received as wages, are all forgotten, and only the true and passionate love for the Steam Road Locomotive remains.

I have noted with pleasure the ever increasing interest in steam on the Rally Fields. The willingness and determined effort, against great odds, to keep it alive, has gladdened my heart.

Talking " Steam " on and off the Rally Ground has made me many friends, and it is thanks to the encouragement of Mr. J. H. Trounson, of the Cornish Tin Mines, and the West of England Steam Engine Society, and to Mr. W. Boddy, of *Motor Sport* that this book has been written.

The stories contained in the following pages are based upon my own experiences, and those of employees in my late father's

Steam Haulage and Engineering business in a small country village on the Surrey-Sussex border. I make no claim for the history of the firm, for it is typical of many hundreds up and down the country, but is merely a basis upon which to weave the stories.

There must be many others better qualified than I to write about working steam on the roads. Nevertheless I sincerely hope my readers will find enjoyment in this book, and gain some idea of what life was like with engines in the early years of this century. I only ask that they will forgive me if I appear to have written my own life history, for it was never intended as such.

JACK   HAMPSHIRE

Contents

List of Illustrations

Halftone plates

Between pp 40 and 41
Marshall portable engine and Burrell sawbench, 1902.
Clayton & Shuttleworth 6 h.p. traction, 1908
Clayton & Shuttleworth traction on road haulage, 1910
Wallis & Steevens traction, 1917

Between pp 56 and 57
Father and his Model T Ford, 1914
Clayton & Shuttleworth's 5-ton tractor
6 h.p. Burrell, built 1892
Aveling & Porter tandem roller loaded on a train

Between pp 104 and 105
Clayton & Shuttleworth 1914 5-ton steam wagon
Foden steam wagon at Aldershot, 1916
Clayton & Shuttleworth 5-ton steam wagon, 1918
Burrell traction at work in 1921

Between pp 120 and 121
The author on his 1916 chaindrive Sunbeam motorcycle
1930 6-ton Foden wagon rescued from a scrapyard
The same wagon after " treatment "

Foreword

Life began for a certain little boy in a Cornish town in the year 1905. The place where he was born was the centre of the Cornish tin mining industry which gave rise to a great deal of heavy haulage and in consequence traction engines, steam wagons and steam rollers were then to be seen on every hand.

Another factor which exerted a powerful influence on the boy's character was that he was born with an incurable addiction to steam power in all its many forms and that is something which medical science is powerless to eradicate ! This tendency, however, was not altogether surprising for the child was a distant relative of the immortal Richard Trevithick, the great pioneer of steam loco- motion by road and rail, and as steam was in the blood it was only natural that at some future date it would again make itself manifest.

In 1905 there were very few motor cars in Cornwall and the motor lorry just did not exist. All light transport depended on the horse, but most large businesses sported a steam wagon or even a fleet of traction engines and in consequence life was very thrilling for the said small boy. His father was the head of a firm which owned two beautifully maintained 5-ton steel tyred Foden steam wagons, and a great friendship grew up between the young enthusiast and the firm's senior driver (who, happily, is still alive). At a tender age the boy was allowed to steer the No. 1 wagon, *Pride of the West*— but only when a policeman was not looking ! The climax of excit- ment came when the firm bought a second-hand 8 horse power Robey road locomotive—but of that ill-starred engine the less said the better ! The local brewery company also owned a fleet of Foden wagons and the boy became so imbued with steam that it was his proud boast that he could identify most of the many local engines by sound alone.

Gradually the years wore on and the boy was sent away to boarding school. Then came the '20's and in those years of rapid change the motor lorry began to appear in numbers and the beloved steam wagons grew fewer and fewer. Next, the local mining in- dustry declined and with it disappeared most of the big road loco- motives. By the outbreak of war in 1939 only a few agricultural traction engines remained in use in the Westcountry and even the magnificent showmen's engines were on the way out. The boy had by now grown to manhood and had had to accept the disappearance of steam from the roads as a part of so-called " progress " and yet, almost unknown to himself, the passing of these grand old machines had left a deep longing in his mind which nothing else could satisfy.

Then, just as it seemed that the beloved " steam " had gone and gone for ever, the traction engine preservation movement burst on the scene and the boy, who had become the adult who is now writing these words, was irresistibly drawn into the movement. Later, he was to become the owner of an engine himself, but the greatest and most unexpected consequence of this renewed interest in steam was the wonderful friendships which he formed and amongst these he is privileged to include that of Jack Hampshire.

Jack is one of those very rare people who has learnt his job the hard way (and nobody who reads this book can doubt how hard a way it was !) but he can also write about it with equal skill, and this is most unusual. Furthermore, he has a delightful sense of humour and an appreciation of the strange and ridiculous. I have had the privilege of reading the stories in this book in manuscript form and they have fascinated me. One and all they are of absorbing interest and many of them are extremely funny. However, throughout the whole of them there is the atmosphere of solid reality and one is left with the feeling that here is an account of what it was like to earn one's living by means of steam on the roads as told by one of the men who lived through it all.

When Jack first suggested that I should write a foreword to this book I shrank from the task; it is one thing to own an engine as a hobby but quite another to have owned and driven a fleet of them under commercial conditions in those hard old days. However, Jack was so persuasive that, against my better judgement, I agreed to have a go in the rather forlorn hope of trying to repay him for some of his many kindnessess to me. Though I am deeply conscious of my inadequacy for this task, I cannot too highly commend this collection of stories to all those who are interested in steam road locomotion and I am confident that this book will soon be found on the shelves of everyone in the traction engine world.

JOHN H. TROUNSON, A.C.S.M., A.M.I.M.M.
Vice-Chairman, West of England Steam Engine Society.
Hon. Curator, Cornish Engines Preservation Society.

Preface

I am delighted that I have been asked to write a Preface to Jack Hampshire's delightful book. The suggestion that he should embark on this task was made after I had read one of his articles in *Steaming*, the Journal of the National Traction Engine Club, and had enjoyed it so much.

Mr. Hampshire contrives to capture the very atmosphere of the nineteen-twenties, when steam was out and about on our roads and on the farms, a force to be respected, long before it was ousted by petrol politics. Because he does not shirk from including details, his book is fascinating; a far more vivid and intimate record of the old days of road haulage and steam threshing than more general histories can ever hope to be. As you read of the Claytons, Burrells, Fodens and Wallis & Steevens that he knew so well, you are projected back delightfully into an age when the roads of this tight little Island were peaceful and comparatively deserted, when time was there a'plenty, when steam traction engines, steam rollers and steam wagons enlivened our youth and the pages of *The Commercial Motor* contained pictures and statistics of fleets of Fodens as well as petrol lorries.

Today diesel fumes replace the aroma of warm oil and coal smoke, the ancient factory buildings of Wallis & Steevens in Basingstoke are threatened by overspill development, and noise and pace and anxiety abound.

How pleasant then to turn the pages of Jack Hampshire's little book and re-live the old days, to read what he has to tell and to be carried back into the leisurely past . . . That this steam enthusiast still drives a steamer today I regard as splendid. That he has found time to put pen to paper is something for which all true advocates of steam should be grateful.

W. BODDY, Editor, *Motor Sport*.

An Historical View

PETWORTH

Novel Sight. On Thursday great wonderment was caused by seeing a steam engine travelling on the turnpike road coming into Petworth. It turned out to be a steam plough and engine going to Stag Park to be used on Lord Leconfield's estate. It travelled along with the greatest ease and seemed to be under perfect control. We hear that it was worked on Saturday, but we were unable to see it's operation.

West Sussex Gazette. 7th. November, 1861.

HORSHAM

A Steam Engine running upon the highway. We have before this heard of a steam carriage running upon our common roads, and we are now enabled to say that we have seen such a machine running about our town; and as far as we could discern, the man at the helm had no difficulty in steering it in any direction he might think proper. The carriage was manufactured by Mr. T. W. Cowan, Kent Iron Works, Greenwich. It's appearance is neat and compact, and it is constructed to carry twelve passengers comfortably, and when painted for our International Exhibition (as we believe it is intended to be), it will be one amongst the many objects of attraction to the visitors. During it's stay at Horsham, several excursions were made with it round about the town, to the amusement and to some extent to the astonishment of the people; and perhaps if we were to add, to the alarm of the horses, we should not be far out.

West Sussex Gazette. 17th April, 1862.

1

How a
steam engine works

FOR THOSE who are not fully conversant with the working parts of a Steam Traction Engine, I propose to give in this chapter a very brief description of the general principles employed in these machines. Though it must be understood that it is a far from comprehensive coverage of the subject, the sole object is to give the reader sufficient knowledge to enable him more readily to understand and enjoy the stories in the following pages.

Should the reader be desirous of learning more about the steam engine, I would recommend him to acquire a text book on the subject, as the primary reason of this publication is to entertain rather than to instruct. For those familiar with the workings of a traction engine, I ask their indulgence for this chapter.

Basically the principles are the same for the Agricultural Traction Engine, Road Locomotive, Portable Engine, and the over-type Steam Wagon, but applied in various forms to suit each particular machine.

In the case of the Steam Wagon there are two kinds. The " Over-Type," and the " Under-Type." For the purpose of this book I propose to deal with the over-type only. For those who are anxious to know the difference between the two, the " Over " is a wagon where the motion, or works, are mounted on top of a loco-motive type boiler. Conversely, with the " Under " a vertical boiler is used, and the motion is mounted in the chassis under the wagon body, the final drive being either by chain or, in the case of the later models, by shaft and worm gear. In the over-type the final drive is by chain.

THE BOILER

Let us first consider the source of the power, the boiler. For the purpose of this book it will be confined to that of the locomotive type. To assist the reader more easily to understand it, an outline drawing of a simple traction engine boiler is given opposite.

It will be seen from the drawing that the boiler consists of two separate parts; the outer shell and the inner fire-box. The inner fire-box is riveted and stayed to the outer fire-box in such a manner as to leave a water space all around between the two. At the bottom of the fire-box is the foundation ring to which are fixed the rests that hold the firebars, or firegrate, in position.

From the top front of the inner fire-box a number of fire-tubes connect through the boiler shell to the front tube plate. These are to carry the hot gases from the fire to the smoke-box fitted at the front end of the boiler shell. As many tubes are used as is practicable in order to obtain the maximum heating area possible for the fire to transfer its heat to the water surrounding them. After the hot gases have reached the smoke-box, they pass up the chimney to discharge into the atmosphere.

THE FUSIBLE PLUG

At the top of the inner fire-box, known as the " Fire-box Crown ", is fitted the " Fusible Plug." This is a safety device against possible damage to the crown by a shortage of water in the boiler. It is a brass plug with a $\frac{3}{8}$ inch hole drilled longitudinally through its centre. This hole is filled with lead and the whole plug is screwed tightly into the crown.

The safety action is as follows: whilst the water in the boiler is high enough to cover the crown on the inside, the lead in the plug will remain intact, but should the water fall for any reason below the correct level, the lead in the plug will melt and steam will blow down through the hole left by the melted lead and extinguish the fire.

This unfortunate occurrence is known as " Dropping the Plug " and is severely frowned upon by the owner of the engine, since the driver ought to know well in advance that the water had

8

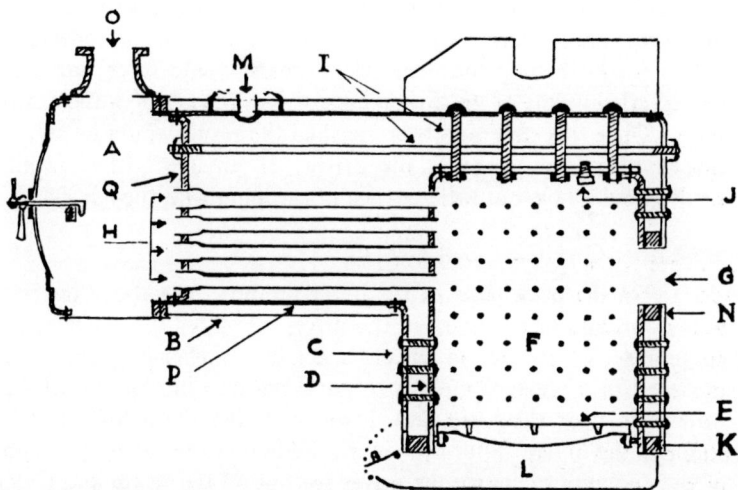

DIAGRAM OF A LOCOMOTIVE TYPE BOILER

KEY

A—Smokebox	J—Fusible Plug
B—Boiler Lagging	K—Foundation Ring
C—Outer Firebox	L—Ashpan & Damper
D—Inner Firebox	M—Steam Outlet to Cylinder
E—Firebars	N—Firehole Ring
F—Firebox	O—Chimney Base
G—Firehole	P—Boiler Shell
H—Fire Tubes	Q—Tube Plate
I—Longitudinal & Crown Stays	

reached the danger level, and should withdraw the fire from the fire-box long before the lead in the plug had melted.

Too much stress cannot be laid upon the efficient working of the fusible plug in any boiler, for should it for any reason repeatedly fail to work, in time the pressure of steam would force the over-heated crown-plate of the fire-box down over the heads of the crown stays. Once this state had been reached the result would be such a catastrophic explosion that the driver, or anyone within several yards, would have but little chance of escaping with their lives.

WATER GAUGE COLUMNS

On the back plate of the outer fire-box, just above the fire-hole door, and in easy view of the driver, are fitted the water gauge columns. These are, in effect, specially toughened glass tubes mounted in a brass column at top and bottom, through which the water can float easily up and down, denoting the actual level of water in the boiler. Shut-off cocks are fitted at the top and bottom of each column to enable the driver to shut off the steam and water in the event of accidental damage to the glass tubes.

Another type used frequently in place of the glass tubes is the Klinger Gauge. This is a brass fitting where a flat glass is used and held in place by a slotted cover plate, with the water fluctuating at the back of the glass. While the reading of the level is not quite so easily seen by the driver as in the former method, the possibility of accidental damage to the glass, or the fittings, is very remote.

STEAM GAUGE

Placed in full view of the driver is the steam gauge, a device denoting the pressure of steam in the boiler. This has a pointer, motivated by the steam pressure, moving over a graduated dial. As the pressure in the boiler fluctuates the pointer moves accordingly, indicating exact pressure in lbs. per square inch. Pressure per square inch, incidentally, means the amount of pressure upon every square inch of surface area inside the whole area of the boiler.

BOILER MUD-DOORS

Every boiler is fitted with three or more mud-doors. These are located near to the corners at the bottom of the outside fire-box shell, just above the foundation ring. These are removed at frequent intervals, enabling the boiler to be flushed through with a strong jet of water, in order to remove the mud picked up from dirty streams, and scale accumulated inside. Neglect of this operation, which should be carried out after every 100 working hours of the engine, can cause great damage to the inside fire-box plates and stays.

SAFETY VALVES

Among the most important fittings to a boiler are the safety valves. These are always mounted on the highest point of the boiler, i.e., the steam chest, or dome. The safety valve assembly consists of two mushroom shaped valves held down on their seats by a cross bar and a heavy tension spring. This spring is so designed as to hold them down until the pressure in the boiler reaches the safety mark, determined by the makers of the engine and known as the " Working Pressure." When this point is reached the spring can no longer hold the valves down since the pressure under them is equal to that of the spring. Therefore any steam generated in excess of this point lifts the valves from their seatings and " Blows Off " into the atmosphere.

ASHPAN AND DAMPER

Since the fire in the fire-box changes the water into steam, it follows that to control the amount of steam generated, the fire must be controlled. For this purpose an ashpan and damper is fitted. This is an airtight box bolted in position under the fire-grate. One side of the box is so hinged that it can be opened or closed at will by the driver from the footplate, enabling him to control the amount of air to the fire, thereby brightening the fire or dampening it.

BOILER FEED PUMP AND INJECTOR

As the steam is used by the engine while it is working, so will the water level in the boiler become correspondingly lower and more water must be put in to replace it. For this purpose two devices can be used, together or separately as the need demands. One is the boiler feed pump, the other is the injector.

Let us consider the feed pump first. It can be driven direct from the engine crank shaft, or through a chain of gears at a slower speed. In either case the reciprocating movement of the pump plunger is obtained through an eccentric and connecting rod. The pump sucks the water from the tank under the foot plate and forces it through a pipe to the boiler clack valve, and thus into the boiler.

BOILER CLACK VALVE

The boiler clack valve is a single valve in a brass casing which is studded to the boiler shell. Its mission is two-fold: first, an assurance against the chance return of water to the pump; the second and much more important function is its automatic shutting off of steam and water from the boiler in the event of accidental fracture of the delivery pipe.

INJECTOR

The injector is a far more delicate instrument than the pump, and much too complicated to be dealt with fully in this chapter. Very briefly, it consists of a series of steam jets and water cones, contained in a brass casing having four openings; 1, the steam inlet, 2, the water inlet, 3, the water delivery outlet to the boiler, 4, the overflow. Usually it is fitted low down on the outside of the tender water tank. Between it and the water tank is a turn cock to control the flow of water into the injector. The steam for operating it is controlled by a wheel valve from a position on the footplate. A pipe runs from the delivery opening of the injector to a separate clack valve on the boiler, as in the case of the pump.

To operate it, the water control cock is first opened, allowing water to flow into the injector. When it runs freely from the overflow, steam is turned on at the wheel valve. According to the degree of pressure in the boiler, so the water control cock is adjusted until the injector is working cleanly, that is, no water is wasting from the overflow. It is then being forced into the boiler.

WATER TANKS

Normally the agricultural traction engine is fitted with one tank only, which is built into the tender under the footplate. On the other hand the road locomotive and the tractor carry an extra supply in what is called the " Belly Tank." This is suspended under the boiler shell, between the front and hind wheels, and is coupled to the tender tank by means of the levelling pipe. The extra supply enables the road locomotive and the tractor to travel greater distances on the road before having to stop and refill.

WATER LIFT

Filling the tanks, or " Picking up Water," as it is referred to, is quite a simple operation and for this purpose a steam water lift is provided. This piece of apparatus is bolted to the top of the tank. At one end is the steam inlet whilst the other end is the outlet to the tank. At the middle section the flexible hose is connected, usually 25 to 30 feet in length.

To pick up water the free end of the hose is lowered into the stream. The steam is then turned on at the wheel valve control. As it reaches the lift it blows through a jet across the opening where the suction hose is joined on, into a cone set immediately opposite. This action creates a vacuum in the body of the lift. Water then rushing up the hose to fill the vacuum is caught by the jet of steam, and blown into the tank. It will continue to flow thus until the tank is full and the steam turned off.

STEAM CHEST

Having dealt with the boiler and its fittings, we must now turn to that part of the engine where the steam is turned into working power, and to begin we will take the steam chest.

This is an extremely complicated casting, housing cylinder, piston, slide valve, governor valve and the regulator valve. To simplify matters, I propose to take the single cylinder first, and deal with compounding later.

The steam chest, sometimes called the steam dome, acts as a receptacle for ' dry ' steam, that is, steam as free of water as the boiler pressure/temperature will allow. That is why the safety valves already referred to are placed at the highest point so that dry steam only is blown off.

The cylinders and slide valve walls are, for the greater part, surrounded by live dry steam. This is done to minimise, to the utmost degree, the condensation of steam in the cylinder when the engine is working, thereby economizing in the consumption of coal and water.

At the top of the steam chest, immediately below the safety valves, is the regulator, or throttle valve. This is coupled to the regulator lever mounted on the breast plate, within easy reach of the driver's hand.

This flat square shaped valve can slide to and fro between guides over a hole below it. Over and around it is live steam. Thus as the regulator lever is moved, the valve slides along and uncovers a portion of the hole below it. The steam then passes down through the hole and is conducted through a tunnel to the slide valve chamber,

13

where it starts its working journey to the open air. In this way the starting, stopping and various speeds of the engine are controlled.

THE "D" SLIDE VALVE

The function of the slide valve is to admit and cut off steam to either end of the cylinder at the right moment. To do this the valve must travel to and fro across the "Valve Port Face." This movement is achieved by an eccentric fixed in position on the crank shaft, so that as the crank shaft rotates the eccentric will move the valve over the port face.

A "D" slide valve is shown in fig. 1., and the valve port face is shown in fig. 2., In fig. 2., the steam port to the front of the piston is marked "F", and the port to the back is marked "B". The centre port "E" is the exhaust port.

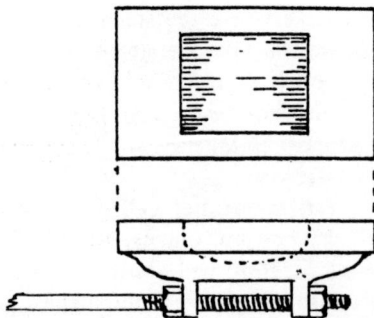

Figure 1—Diagram showing the shape of a "D" slide valve.

For clarity we will assume the engine to be running in a clockwise direction, with one eccentric only. Upon examination of fig. 3, it will be seen that the piston is at the back of the cylinder, and the valve has opened the port "B". The admission of steam through this port will push the piston forward, thus through the piston rod, crosshead, and connecting rod it will thrust the crank round one half turn. Before the piston has completed its full stroke, however, the valve will have travelled back, cutting off the supply of steam to port "B" and leaving the steam that is left in the cylinder to push the piston the remainder of its stroke by expansion.

When the piston has reached the full extent of its stroke, the valve will have moved to a point where the port "F" will be un-

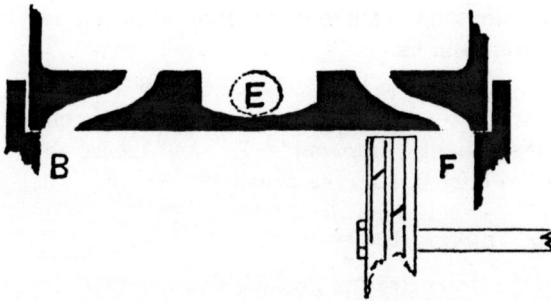

Figure 2—Diagram of a valve port face showing exhaust opening and steam ports to cylinder.

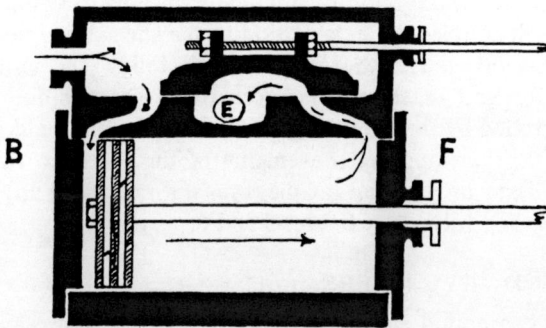

Figure 3—Diagram showing the slide valve and piston positions at the beginning of the forward stroke.

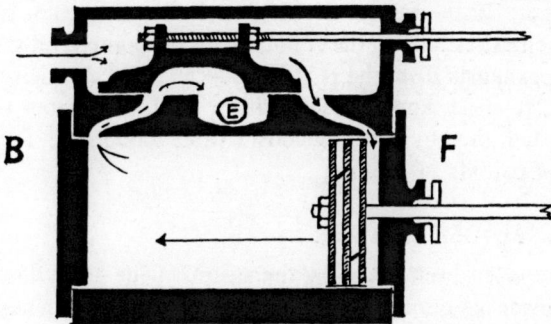

Figure 4—The slide valve and piston positions at the beginning of the backward stroke.

covered, thus admitting steam to the front of the piston, and thereby pushing it back, as in fig. 4.

In this position the " D " shaped hollow in the face of the valve will have uncovered port " B " on the inside, allowing the expended steam to pass into port " E " and thence through the exhaust pipe to discharge up the chimney.

THE LINK MOTION

To make the engine run in either direction two eccentrics are fixed at specific angles to the crank on the crank shaft, one for the forward motion and the other for reverse. Each is connected by a rod to the Stevenson Sliding Link Gear, one to the top of the link and one to the bottom. As the link is able to swing on the " Die " which couples the link motion to the slide valve, raising or lowering the link causes the slide valve to follow the motion of either the forward or the reverse eccentric. The position of the link is controlled by the Reversing Lever from the footplate. In the mid position, the opposing movements of the eccentric rods will cause the link to oscillate on the die, thus not imparting any movement to the slide valve. See figures 5 and 6.

COMPOUND CYLINDERS

The compound engine works in exactly the same way as the single cylinder engine, but is fitted with two cylinders, one larger than the other. The smaller is the " High Pressure ", and the larger the " Low Pressure ", the object being to use the steam twice, by its own expansion. In the case of the single cylinder, the steam is used once, and then exhausted up the chimney. In the compound system, as the steam exhausts from the H.P. cylinder, it is led through to the L.P. slide valve chest, and is used again in the L.P. cylinder before being exhausted, thereby effecting considerable economy in fuel and water in long periods of running.

NOMINAL HORSE POWER

I have often been asked by the steam engine enthusiast how the horse power, as quoted by the makers of traction engines, was arrived at. Briefly it was a legacy left to us by James Watt, who needed some means of comparing the power of the mining engines built by him with the power of a horse. After repeated experiments

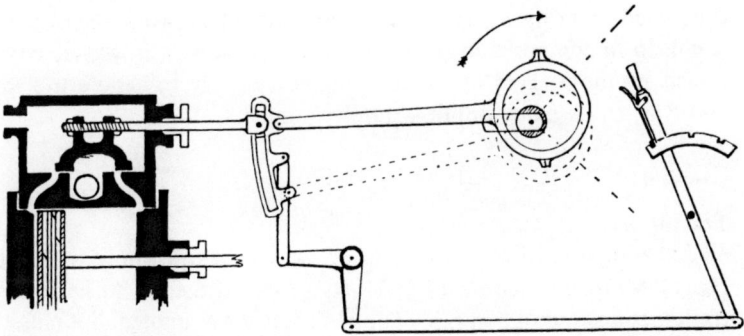

Figure 5—The Stevenson link motion with the link set to bring the forward eccentric into full action.

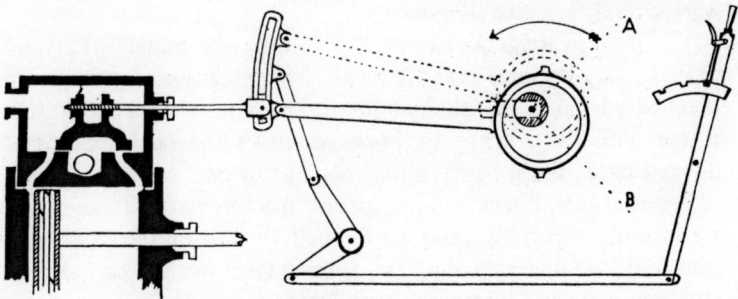

Figure 6—The link motion with the backward eccentric in full action. The dotted lines A. B. indicate the position of the eccentrics in relation to the crank.

his idea was accepted by most engine builders of that day, and was used in the realms of the traction world, though it was soon realised that his standard was incorrect as far as the traction engine was concerned, bearing no relation to the amount of work the engine could do in comparision to that of a horse. It was, however, continued by the makers of traction engines, merely to denote a size, and was, as its name implies, purely nominal.

CLASSIFICATION OF ENGINES

Tractor

A light road locomotive which was built to comply with the Heavy Motor Car Order of 1904, to a limit of 5 tons, to haul one trailer, at a speed of 5 m.p.h. The H.P. was never quoted, but classification was by tonnage. A tractor was normally designed with compound cylinders, fitted with flywheel brake, hind wheel brakes, roping drum, differential locking gear, 3 speed gears, two injectors, water lift, and belly tank.

Heavy Road Locomotive

Built in weights of from 10 to 20 tons. Nominal H.P. from 5 to 10. Legally hauling three trailers and a water cart at a speed limit of 4 m.p.h. Normally spring mounted back and front, on steel tyres, but latterly on rubber tyres as tarred roads came into being. Compound Cylinders. Fitted with three-speed gears, differential locking gear, flywheel brake, and hind wheel brakes, boiler feed pump, two injectors, water lift, and belly tank.

Agricultural Traction Engine

Built in weights of from 9 to 15 tons. Nominal H.P. from 5 to 8. Mostly in single cylinder form. Nearly always unsprung. Iron shod wheels, made to take paddles or spuds for use on soft ground. Fitted with band brake to work on either the back axle or the intermediate shaft, governors, roping drum, two-speed gears, differential gear, boiler feed pump, one injector, water lift, and tender water tank. Specially designed for belt work from the flywheel for threshing, sawmilling, baling and general farm work. Used extensively by farmers and threshing contractors.

Steam Wagon

Virtually a lorry propelled by steam. Graded in tonnages, and not in h.p.'s, i.e., 3, 5 and 6-ton wagons. Fitted with high speed engines, compound cylinders incorporating a double high pressure gear. Usually with three speed gear. Chain drive from the second motion shaft to the rear axle. Chain steerage to front axle. Speed limit on rubber tyres 8 miles per hour, later models fitted with " Ackerman " steerage (car type) and internal expanding brakes to hind wheels. Speed limit increased to 16 m.p.h., later to 20 m.p.h. All models carried a boiler feed pump and one injector. All wagons could legally haul one trailer.

The steam wagons mentioned in the following stories were of the early type, fitted with two-speed gears, chain steerage, and subject to a speed limit of 8 m.p.h.

The Portable Engine

An engine that is not self propelled. Used for semi-stationary work. Mounted on iron or wooden wheels for transportation. Drawn by horses in the early days, latterly by traction engine or other means. Made in a great variety of powers, from 1½ h.p. up-wards, in single, double high pressure, and compound cylinders. Some fitted with boiler feed pump only, others carried an injector as well.

Father's first engine the Marshall portable on its way to Petworth. (*Drawing by Miss A. Child and the author*).

2

How it all began
— by accident

OF COURSE there must be a beginning to all things, even to starting up a business where the steam engine plays a leading role. Though how Father got mixed up with it was more by accident than design, for he knew as much about steam as steam knew about him, which I assure you was but little.

It was only by rummaging through some old papers one day that I stumbled upon a clue, contained in some letters that were once the property of my father, as to how our family business of haulage contractors and engineers came into being.

In the year 1898, just before my people found me under a gooseberry bush, father was the licensee of a pub at Cowes in the Isle-of-Wight. According to information gleaned from the letters it seems that among father's many failings was his apparent fondness for oysters, and through a surfeit of these, he was almost laid low with typhoid.

You are asking, as well you may, what all this has to do with steam. Well, briefly, nothing. It is only to emphasize that when " Old Devil Steam Bug " starts working on you anything can happen.

On doctor's orders father had to go inland, well away from the sea, to convalesce. Thus it came to be that he found himself installed in a pretty little pub on the banks of the River Arun, in a tiny village in Sussex.

Father was a tall man, generous by nature, and with a wonderful sense of humour. Quickly he made friends with all the local lads

21

and was soon caught up in their country activities including his favourite sport, rabbit shooting. This pastime was destined to bring him into the land of steam.

He was out shooting one day with one of his new found friends, when at noon, finding themselves close to a village inn and desperately in need of refreshment, they went in and, I regret to say, imbibed a little too freely.

According to records, an auction sale of farm machinery was held that day near the inn, and in very jovial mood that afternoon the two friends found themselves standing in a group of would-be bidders. Father, with his cap at a rakish angle, full of good cheer and home brewed cider, stood gently swaying to and fro in the autumn breeze, occasionally rubbing the tip of his nose, a most unfortunate habit of his as the auctioneer took this for a bidding sign. Before father knew what was happening, down went the auctioneer's gavel with a bang, and an old 6 h.p. single cylinder Marshall portable steam engine and sawbench were knocked down to " The gentleman in the cloth cap."

Soon a veritable battle of words ensued between him and the auctioneer. Father, with a great variety of gesticulations and expletives, vowed that he had not made a bid. The auctioneer, of course, vehemently argued otherwise, to the great delight of all present, as they crowded round determined not to miss a moment of the fun.

This little interlude was brought to an abrupt end by an old chap with a large shaggy beard and wearing a battered billy-cock hat, stepping between the two. Looking up into Father's face he said, " I don't know who you be, Sir. but if you'll listen to me you'll keep 'er. I'll work 'er for 'ee, an' make 'er pay".

Father scrutinized the old chap through half closed eyes for a moment, then blurted out, " And what the hell do you know about it ? " " Well Sir " said the old man, touching his hat in salute, " I bin workin' of 'er these last fifteen yers, an' she's a good 'un."

I can only suppose that it was old Harry Puddick's honest pleading, for that is who the old fellow turned out to be, which persuaded father to acknowledge his purchase of the Marshall and the sawbench. This momentary decision of father's took him into the land of steam, a thing he knew absolutely nothing at all about, and which was to change his life completely.

It transpired that Harry, faithful to his word, and with the help of two employees, ran the set of sawing tackle with such success that three years later it induced father to migrate from the Isle-of-Wight to Loxwood to manage the business himself. That was how it all began. Old devil steam bug had won, all hands down.

On further perusal of the ledger kept by Harry in 1898, and of the letters, I learned that the first sawing contract with the Marshall under father's name, was for the Leconfield Estate, at Petworth, and that six horses were hired to haul the engine and sawbench from the site of the sale to Petworth.

It was interesting to read that the carter in charge of the team of horses was fined five shillings for damage to the Queen's highway, to wit, Fox Hill, by the use of a skid-pan on the back wheel of the engine going down the hill.

I have no record of the Marshall's number, alas, I can only tell you that she was built about the year 1880. The sawbench was built by Burrell's of Thetford, about the same year, and took a 4 foot 6 inch circular saw.

I remember the old Marshall even now, as from boyhood to manhood she was always my pet. At the early age of eight my Saturdays and holidays from school were spent tending and driving her under the guiding hand of old Harry. Though having steam in my blood, as I did, I needed but little guiding. I think it is worth recording that she worked for our firm unfailingly until 1920. That goes for Harry too, for he stayed with the firm the rest of his working life, nearly twenty five years, as a sawyer.

The last time I saw the old Marshall working was in our own yard. For some reason her boiler shell had become so thin under the steam chest, that it was somewhat disconcerting to see steam spurt from under it from either end when she was pulling hard, although her working pressure was only 80 lbs. per square inch. For safety reasons she really had to be taken out of service, although her inner fire-box was in a remarkably good condition, thanks to having burned wood all the time.

Ah well, I suppose there must be an end, as well as a beginning to all things, even to an old portable steam engine.

23

3

The new venture:
Threshing

SOON AFTER father had taken up residence in Loxwood he sensed that there was an opening for threshing in the surrounding district. Seeing an advertisement in a daily paper offering a set of threshing tackle for sale, he made his mind up there and then to put his theory into action.

Since he knew absolutely nothing at all about threshing machines or steam engines, he enlisted the help of an employee of a local engineering firm at Wisborough Green to make a survey of the set of tackle for him.

As it was now necessary to travel around the district to pay the sawing gang, and to measure up the timber they converted each week, he soon began to realize that in a country area some form of transport a little more comfortable than a bicycle was desperately needed. He acquired for himself a high-stepping horse and dog-cart; at this period he was hardly aware of the fact that there was such a new-fangled machine on the road as the motor car. However, after an exchange of telegrams between the vendor of the threshing set and himself, he and the engineer set out for Witley in the dog cart.

The survey seems to have been satisfactory for in due course after a settlement in golden sovereigns as was the practice of those days, Father became the owner of a 7 h.p. Ransomes Simms and Jeffries single cylinder portable engine, a 4 foot 6 inch drum Clayton and Shuttleworth machine, and a Wallis and Steevens elevator.

Later the set was hauled from Witley to Loxwood, a distance of roughly twenty miles, by a team of horses.

This new venture, of course, meant three more employees on the staff, now making a total of six. I simply cannot refrain from quoting their names. There was the driver who came with the engine. His name was Lew Ayler and he was known to all and sundry as " Mouse." He was short, very thick set and perpetually as black as the ace of spades by continual contact with oil and wood smoke. His lower lip had a permanent droop on one side caused by the constant use of a short black clay pipe. I don't remember ever seeing him without it, in fact I am convinced that he slept with it in this position.

The other two were local men. One was Elias Potter, known as " Spinner." He was the feeder on the machine. The other was Tobias Nash, who needless to say was called " Toby." Both these characters wore corduroy trousers tied with string under the knee, and heavy hard woven jackets fitted with an inside pocket extending the whole of the way round the bottom of the jacket ; the kind of pocket known in most country districts as a " Poacher's Pocket." For these two celebrities it was a most essential fitting for their garments. They were exceedingly expert in the use of the catapult and were numbered among the best poachers in the area, and they made up their beer money, as they preferred to call it, by the casual sale of rabbits, hares, and the odd pheasant. Typical country lads, they were wonderful workers, with hearts as big as barn doors and with thirsts in proportion. Their staple food appeared to be bread and cheese, and beer; on this simple diet they throve wonderfully.

Mouse, I regret to say, did not remain in our employ for more than three years. He died chiefly by neglect of himself. He was, as were indeed most of the threshing types of that day, somewhat allergic to soap and water. Most of them it seems, even if they had a home, preferred to live rough. They spent their evenings either in the nearest pub or poaching, then crawled back to the barn to sleep in the straw for the rest of the night, wherever the tackle happened to be.

Poor old Mouse met his end one day by walking under the driving belt of the machine whilst it was still running. He was hit on the head by the belt fastener. He died a fortnight later of septicaemia. He was working the day before his death and was found by his mates the next morning dead in the straw.

Threshing in those days was, as indeed it always has been, a filthy job, for immediately the machine started up a cloud of dust and thistle-down surrounded the tackle on all sides for many yards, and only the very hardy could work with it for long periods. The driver of the engine was the only one to escape it if the wind was in the right direction, but heaven help him if it blew contrawise. My experience of the threshing gangs in the early days showed me that they were, beyond all doubt, a tough bunch.

The gang, as far as the contractor was concerned was as follows: the engine driver, who was responsible for the complete set of tackle and its running ; the feeder, whose job it was to feed the sheaves of corn into the drum mouth of the machine; and the sackman, who attended to the sacks hanging under the corn chutes. These when full, he would take off the hooks holding them, replace them with empties, and wheel the full sacks to a pile where they would later be loaded on to a farm cart to be taken to the granary. For every full sack taken off he would make a chalk mark on the tally slate. This was most important as the price for the threshing was based upon the number of sacks threshed out.

The rest of the gang was paid and supplied by the farmer. It consisted of two men on the corn rick to pitch the sheaves to the top of the thresher ; a bond cutter, usually the farm boy, whose job it was to cut the bond with a long curved bond-knife, and to pass the sheaf to the feeder ; two men to build the straw rick, and one to rake away the cavings, or chaff, i.e., the husk of the grain of wheat, barley, or oats, etc. These men, with the exception of the rick builders were mostly casual labourers who would follow the threshing set from farm to farm throughout the season, and who generally " slept rough " with the rest of the gang.

All this, I would remind you, was between the years 1900 and 1910. With the advent of the first world war conditions were vastly improved, the traction engine became more widely used and a living van was provided for the use of the driver, feeder and the sackman.

The farmer also supplied the coal and water for the engine, the latter coming mostly from the duck-pond which was invariably so full of weed, mud and tadpoles that it necessitated washing out the boiler practically every week to keep it free of impurities. It was also part of the farmer's contract to supply the necessary horses to haul the tackle from his farm to the next site.

He was also expected, though it was not specified on his contract, to supply refreshment for the day, which invariably took the form of bread and cheese with beer or home made cider. Sometimes, if in charitable mood, he would hand round a glass of home made wine at the end of the day, and on occasions this had disastrous results, according to its potency.

By 1904 father found it virtually impossible, to cope with the amount of threshing in the area with one set of tackle, and in due course he bought another set, this time from an estate near Reigate. This set consisted of a Marshall 6 h.p. single cylinder portable, a Marshall 4 foot 6 inch drum machine with a trusser fitted to the shaker mouth. As all horses on the farms had their names, so had the engines, and this one bore the name of "Duchess." For the uninitiated, a trusser is a piece of machinery that receives the straw as it comes from the shaker mouth, and ties it with string into ½ cwt. trusses. After it is tied the truss rolls down a ramp, is picked up by a man with a prong and is pitched to the rick builders, no mean feat when the rick has reached beyond shoulder height.

Speaking of heavy work, it was no picnic to set a portable engine to a machine, especially if the ground was soft, as most farm stack yards were. To "set to", it was necessary to line the flywheel up to the drum pulley at just the right distance from the machine to enable the driving belt to be put on. The engine generally weighed five or six tons, and bottle screw jacks had to be used to lift and strike the engine over to the exact position. This was often done in mud, reaching up to, or even over, the tops of one's boots.

It was through this kind of thing that father got down to serious thinking in terms of a traction engine. One of the threshing gangs, when trying to get the engine set to the machine, got so bogged down that after three days of toiling a team of timber hauling horses had to be called in. With the aid of the horses and a set of double purchase pulley blocks they were able to extricate the engine from the muddy hole.

This episode, coupled with the difficulty of getting enough horses at times to haul the set to another farm, brought father to the conclusion that a traction engine was by far the better proposition.

So it came about that in the autumn of 1907 he placed an order with Clayton and Shuttleworth of Lincoln for a new 6 h.p. single cylinder, two-speed agricultural traction engine to be built, fitted with a geared-down feed pump, governors, and an extra large

27

roping drum. This engine on completion was exhibited at the Royal Counties Show in the summer of 1908 at Chichester. After the show she was delivered to us at Loxwood, a gleaming beauty in show colours and lining. She was, in every way, a truly magnificent engine.

What a red letter day it was in my young life, then at the ripe age of eight, and I am quite sure, in that of father's too, when for the first time in his life he climbed into the tender of his own traction engine and under the guiding hand of Clayton's driver instructor steered her home. What a day to celebrate, and the celebrations were worthy of the occasion !

With the growing amount of machinery the problems of maintenance became more acute, for drivers in those distant days although good drivers, were far from engineers, and beyond packing a gland or tightening a nut they were out of their depth. For any major or minor repair a firm of engineers at Wisborough Green had to be called in. Father had forseen this trouble and to prepare against it had placed my elder brother Cyril with this firm as an apprentice. About six months after the new Clayton traction engine arrived home, he had completed his apprenticeship and came home to work in father's business as a steam engineer.

It is as strange to me as it must be to my reader that father, from the day he bought his first engine at the auction sale till the day he died, knew less than nothing about a steam engine. He had no mechanical knowledge whatever. The only thing he could or would do was to steer a traction engine, or light a fire in one. But believe me, he was an astute business man.

I think this incident was typical of him. He had been interviewing a man who had applied for a driver's job, and after the formal questions had been asked he enquired, " Have you ever dropped a fusible plug ? " " No, Sir " came the prompt reply. " Have you ever had an engine over on its side, or in the ditch ? " " No, Sir, never." "Well," said father, " if you have never experienced this, then how can you be qualified to prevent it happening to one of my engines ? However, here is your fare and five shillings to get some food and a drink to help you on your way."

I always thought it was a bit hard on the chap to have that said to him, but that was father. Nevertheless, five shillings was a lot of money in those days, nearly half a week's wages, so I suppose the poor fellow was compensated to some extent.

4

Drivers come, and drivers go

BY THE YEAR 1910, father had three sets of sawing tackle working full-time on various large estates, each being driven by a portable engine. Periodically one or other of these sets would have to be moved to another site and, although the Clayton traction was bought ostensibly for threshing, she was now playing a part in road-haulage by the transportation of a set of sawing tackle whenever necessary. This led to other haulage jobs, and one I have in mind of the very early days was that of hauling large rag stones from a quarry near Fittleworth to various stretches of road under the Petworth Rural District Council, for road-building and resurfacing. The stone was dumped at intervals of roughly 100 yards on the side of the road in eight to ten ton heaps, later to be broken with stone hammers by hand, mostly by casual labour on piece work.

It was on this job that the driver, Jack Singleton, known as " Hell-fire Jack " because of his merciless treatment of an engine in the matter of speed (unknown to father, of course), after loading twenty-yards of stones into the two traction trucks, pulled out of the Quarry to the nearest pub. Having consumed several pints of a strong ale apiece, Jack, Ted Barnett (the steersman), and the two truck brakemen, clambered up to their respective stations—Jack opening the regulator to career along at eight miles an hour in true " Hell-fire Jack " tradition.

After a mile or so along the road they were met by a gentle-man on horse-back. Jack pulled up to let him pass, but the horse had other ideas, and, rearing and snorting, it nearly unseated its rider. Ted got down from the steering seat to lead the animal by, as was the practice, but the alchohol, by this time having taken charge of his legs—with his cap awry and his knees sagging—made him totally unable to reach it.

The rider, realising the men's condition, yelled to Jack, " You are all drunk and not fit to be in charge." To which Jack retorted, " An' you can't ride that —— 'orse guv'ner ; why the hell don't you ride inside 'im ? You'd be a —— sight safer ! "

During the time these insults were being hurled back and forth, Ted had somehow managed to crawl back to the steering seat. Seeing him there Jack opened the regulator and, with terrific " barks" from the exhaust, the engine trundled off. The horse, already frightened, jumped into the air and shot past the engine like a thunderbolt, mercifully with its rider still on its back. This incident was reported to the police by the horseman and father later had to pay Jack's fine of ten shillings.

About half-a-mile further along, the strong ale had really got hold of Ted (the steersman) inasmuch as he let the front wheel of the engine touch the grass verge at the side of the road. " Hell-fire Jack," being equally " under the weather," did not see the situation in time to stop or to ease up, and in seconds the engine was truly in the ditch.

After viewing the state-of-affairs, in a drunken stupor, all four of them decided to sleep it off. It was in this somnolent position that the Surveyor chanced to find them and promptly sent a telegram to father to inform him of what had happened. When he saw for himself the complete shambles, he nearly had a fit. " Hell-fire Jack," needless to say, was sacked on the spot.

The task of getting the engine out of the ditch fell to my brother Cyril who, until another driver could be found, had to take over the Clayton from " Hell-fire Jack."

Meanwhile, the haulage side of the business was developing so rapidly that in the November of 1910, at the Agricultural Fat Stock Show in London, father placed an order with Chas. Burrell and Sons, of Thetford, for a 5-ton three-speed tractor, fitted with two injectors, roping drum, Pickering governors, belly tank and a three-quarter length cab, to be delivered to us by August 1911. At the same time he ordered from William Tasker and Sons, of Andover, a new tractor trailer.

Until this period all our tackle had been kept in a field with no cover at all, and it became all too apparent that other more suitable accommodation would have to be found. Eventually father bought a house with sufficient ground attached to make a yard big enough to take several engines and machines, together with a large shed and workshops, at Alfold—a village on the Surrey/Sussex border.

To make the foundations of the yard, many tons of sandstone were hauled from the Hascombe Stone Quarries. It was on this job that my brother Cyril, still with the Clayton traction from which " Hell-fire Jack " had been sacked, met his first load of trouble whilst driving an engine.

After loading twenty-tons of stone into the two trucks, he brought the train out on to the main road. Changing the engine into fast gear, he drove on to the top of Hascombe Hill, a long, steep incline, running through a cutting with high banks on either side.

At the top of the hill he stopped, taking the precaution of changing into low gear before descending. The method of gear change on this particular model of Clayton was by a lever sliding over a quadrant fixed to the breast-plate, with a pin to drop into the appropriate hole of the gear selected. Whilst the engine was pulling, the pin would stay in position, but on the over-run it was prone to work out and, if unnoticed, she would slide herself out of gear. This untrustworthy change system was modified after the occurrence of the following incident.

This is precisely what happened a few moments after Cyril had left the hill-top. The first intimation he had that something was wrong, was when he saw that the flywheel had stopped and that the engine was gaining speed. Realising in a flash what had gone amiss, he grabbed the steering wheel from the steersman's hand and shouted to him to jump for it. This he did with alacrity, but not far enough to clear the on-coming front wheel of the first truck. In jumping, he stumbled, and the wheel caught his foot, crushing it to pulp.

Cyril was unaware of this at the time, since he was too preoccupied with steering the engine into the bank in an effort to check the runaway.

At last the engine and trucks came to a halt, but not before she had climbed well up the bank, going over on one side to the actual point of balance, so near, in fact, that two chains had to be

Cyril meets disaster on Hascombe Hill with the Clayton traction.

(Drawing by Miss A. Child and the author).

32

fixed from the hind wheel to a tree further up the bank to prevent her from going right over. So great was the angle, that a horse and brougham coming up the hill could not pass between the Clayton's chimney and the bank of the opposite side. It was the occupants of the brougham who rendered assistance to the injured steersman and carried him to the nearest doctor.

The bank was eventually dug away from under the wheels, while the engine was held up by " jacks " and timbers, to be lowered bit by bit as the earth was cleared. Cyril remained with the Clayton for some weeks as driver, before returning to the yard in his capacity as fitter, after father had acquired another driver.

Although drivers were plentiful in those days, it was extremely hard to find a good one for, although their references were to all intents quite good, the "honest and sober " part of it seemed most inappropriate in a great number of cases. There was an excuse at times, I suppose, for going " off the rails " a little, since father was inclined to be a hard task master. He would be in the yard at six every morning and expected everyone else to be there too. His orders for the day invariably contained enough work to last for twelve hours, and no overtime was paid. In fairness to him though, not one of his employees in sickness or distress ever wanted for anything, especially at Christmas time. Most of our men received a home-cured ham or a brace of pheasants on this festive occasion.

In July of 1911, the new Burrell tractor was sent by rail from Thetford to Billingshurst Station, to be driven from there to our yard by Burrell's instructor. Cyril was appointed her driver, his place in the yard as fitter now being filled by a fellow from Guildford named Bob Hooker.

The new driver for the Clayton, a chap by the name of " Chips " Carpenter, turned out to be another who honoured the Shrine of Bacchus for, during his first fortnight, in a semi-drunken state, he dropped the plug whilst threshing. This misdeed he managed somehow to keep from father by screwing a $\frac{3}{8}$ inch bolt into the hole where the lead should have been. He apparently ran for several weeks like this until, moving from another farm one day, he experienced some difficulty in keeping a head of steam. Quickly the problem grew worse, till finally he had to give up and pull the whole set of tackle on to a wide grass verge. Not knowing what was wrong, he sent the steersman back to the yard for help.

33

"What's the trouble?" enquired father from the Office window, as Bill Hill the steersman entered the yard.

"I dunno, Guv'nor," replied Bill, "but she's poppin' an' crackin' an' smokin' like 'ell."

Bob Hooker, the fitter, was sent out to investigate the trouble.

"What's gone wrong, Chips?" asked Bob on reaching the engine.

"Can't rightly say," replied Chips, " but she won't steam no 'ow."

Bob climbed into the tender, opened the fire-hole door and peered into the fire-box.

"Looks to me as if you're short of water," said Bob. "She's showin' 'alf a glass full," said Chips.

Bob opened the blowdown cock of the gauge column. Nothing came out but steam. "You —— old fool!" said Bob, "She's bone dry—your bottom column is choked up!"

Later, when Bob got into the fire-box to expand the over-heated tubes and to check on the fusible plug, he discovered the $\frac{3}{8}$ inch bolt which Chips had screwed into it. When father heard of this he nearly went mad, and Chips was dismissed on the spot.

The morning following Chips' sacking, I was sitting at my desk in school and was startled by the master informing me that my father wished to see me. Searching my brain for some misdeed I had committed, I walked out to meet him.

"Get your cap, boy," said father, "I've got a job for you to do."

"Do you think the lad can do it?" enquired the master.

"Do it?" said father. "He'll do it a damn sight better than the fellow I've just sacked."

Having no idea what all this was about, I picked up my cap, and followed him out.

So it came to be that at the age of twelve I drove the Clayton traction from where she stood on the grass verge to the farm, about three miles away, where we were to thresh, with father acting as steersman for me. With only two awkward shunts I managed to set the engine to the machine. Father and the feeder put the driving belt on for me, and as proud as a king I completed the first day's threshing. The next day Bob Hooker took over the engine for the day's work, but I was called from school again to shift the set of tackle to the next farm.

34

The next driver father found to replace Chips was a man named Bert Ewings, who turned out to be one of the best we ever had. He stayed with the firm for many years before retiring.

During the first few years of the traction engine's being introduced into the business, father seemed to get more than his full quota of " duff " drivers. Nevertheless, he quickly learned how to sort the " bits " from the " pieces ", as it were, and the driver situation improved considerably, with the odd exception of course.

It seemed to me in those far-off days that beer was as necessary to a driver as water was to an engine. I suppose it must have been, for they drank enough of it, God bless 'em.

5

It's all in a day's work

WITH THE coming of the Burrell tractor, the haulage side of the business grew rapidly, everyone being most impressed by her speed and performance—all and sundry declaring they had never seen the like before. I'm not surprised, for I believe we were the first to own a Burrell three speed tractor in Sussex. Her power and behaviour were truly magnificent.

Sitting at our table at home one evening, I was surprised to see father produce a map and spread it out before him. After studying it in silence for a minute or two, he looked up at my brother and asked, " Have you ever been to London, Cyril ? "

" Yes dad," answered Cyril.

" Do you know your way about there ? " he enquired.

" No ", replied Cyril truthfully.

" Then you had better take this map and study it, for you will be going up there with the Burrell tractor next week."

" What on earth for ? " enquired Cyril.

" There are several loads of special paving stone to be brought down from Little St. James' Street, to Loxwood House, so get to know that map."

So it came to be that at half-past-four on a lovely July morning in 1912, Cyril left for London with the Burrell tractor and trailer, with " Cocky " Strudwick as his mate.

Father was, as usual, in the yard to see Cyril off for, no matter

36

at what hour in the morning an engine would be leaving, he would always be there to see it away.

As Cyril was about to pull out of the yard, father gave him the final details of the job, adding casually, " It's only forty-five miles each way, you should be home again in eighteen hours." Poor Cyril ! Not knowing his way beyond Kingston-on-Thames, or the remotest idea of where he would be able to pick up water en-route, left with high hopes and a doubt in his mind about the eighteen hours.

Midnight came, but no Cyril. " Damn the boy," said father impatiently. " Where the hell's he got to ? I want him to take a load of bricks to Haslemere tomorrow."

At nine o'clock the next morning, as Cyril pulled into the yard, father was pacing to and fro like a caged tiger. " Where the blazes have you been all night ? " he enquired. Cyril looked at him through tired eyes for a moment, " I lost my way in London a time or two," he answered, ignoring father's apparent wrath.

" How the devil could you," said father sternly, " you had a map with you."

" I know," said Cyril, " But that didn't tell me where I could pick up water—I ran out twice. The first time I was able to get some from a pub, the second time I took it from a horse trough and got caught by a policeman whilst taking it." Father's only reply to this was " Damn."

" That's not all," continued Cyril, " Cocky got pinched too."
" What in the name of creation for ? " asked father.

Cyril pondered a moment before answering. " Well, it's like this, whilst I was explaining to the copper how necessary it was that I should have water for the engine, Cocky got a bit impatient and shouted out ' run over his —— toe Cyril, or he'll keep us 'ere all night, and I want to get 'ome.' The copper then pinched him, for inciting me to commit an offence against an officer of the law."

This piece of information left father, for the moment, absolutely speechless. When he did regain his self-control he rasped out, " For heaven's sake the pair of you, go up to the house, have a wash and something to eat, and get to hell out of it to Haslemere before I sack you both."

During the time the paving stone job was in progress, father had taken on a contract to dismantle an old windmill that stood on the south bank of the Wey and Arun Junction Canal. The mill had to be taken to pieces very carefully and each piece had to be marked and numbered. The small parts and the machinery had to be put into crates, and the centre shaft and sweeps transported on a timber tug to London docks for shipment to America.

This meant loading with windmill parts, journeying to London Docks, crossing London to Little St James' Street to load paving stones, and back to Loxwood House. Father now allowed Cyril two days for the round trip—each day representing twelve to fourteen working hours.

With the last load of paving stones having been brought down, Father expected the two remaining journeys to the London Dock to be done in one day for each load. With the last load he gave Cyril instructions to call at Wonersh Park, near Guildford, on his return from London, to pick up a rack saw bench and a push saw bench, that would already be dismantled by the mill gang, and transport it to Hook Park, near Southampton, and return to Wonersh Park after unloading the sawmilling plant for the 8 h.p. Clayton portable engine that was used for driving the sawmill.

Having overnight heard my father giving Cyril detailed orders regarding the Hook Park journey, I decided that since it was summer holidays from school I would go too, as a stowaway.

Quietly I waited in my bedroom till all was still, then stealthily creeping down stairs to the kitchen I cut myself a huge chunk of boiled bacon, a piece of cheese, and the bottom part of a cottage loaf. All this I put into my school bag, then silently made my way back to my bedroom to wait father's calling of Cyril in the morning.

I assure you there was no need for me to worry about oversleeping for when father called anyone the whole household was awakened by his banging on a large gong at the foot of the stairs. My mother and my sister frequently remonstrated with him upon his behaviour in the early hours, but all to no avail, for when father was up the whole world as far as he was concerned had to be up as well.

Realising that my parents would be wondering what in the world had happened to me when I did not appear at the normal hour for breakfast, I left a note for them on my pillow. It was terse, and to the point—" Have gone with Cyril and the Burrell tractor."

At five o'clock in the morning father's hell's tattoo on the gong roused the whole household, as usual, from their slumbers. Quickly I dressed, and waited for the sound of Cyril returning from the yard, after lighting the fire in the Burrell. When at last I heard his footsteps on the path at the back of the house, I shot out of the front door and ran like a hare down to the yard and stowed myself away in the trailer under a cloth.

There I lay until Cyril stopped to pick up water at Halfway Bridge, between Petworth and Midhurst. How it was I was never trodden on by four of the sawmill gang, who were riding with the load, I will never know, for they came exceedingly close to it at times.

It was when Cyril stopped for water and I considered we were far enough from home for me not to be compelled to walk back, that I revealed my presence. It was a very cross and startled Cyril, who upon seeing me shouted angrily " What, in the name of thunder are you doing here ? I suppose you realise we will not be home until tomorrow night." " Yes," I answered sheepishly, " but I've brought enough food to last me." This remark brought a loud guffaw from the sawmill gang.

" What about father ? " he enquired, " does he know you are with me ? " " No," I admitted, and explained about the note I had left on my pillow. " Well," said Cyril thoughtfully, " I suppose there is nothing for it but for you to come along—though I'll guarantee you will not be able to sit down in comfort for a week by the time father has finished with you when we get back." This thought did not worry me a lot just then, but what happened to me upon our return was just as my brother had predicted, and far too painful to be reminded of.

Being able now to ride in the open on the trailer with the sawing gang, all was going well until we reached Petersfield. Here, for some reason, the police seemed to have a great dislike of the traction engine in those far off days, for as we approached the railway level-crossing a policeman stepped into the road and stopped us. Producing his note book and pencil he proceeded to write therein that Cyril was committing a grave offence by allowing thick black smoke to emerge from the chimney. Though just how this could be, since we were using Welsh smokeless coal, was to Cyril and the rest of the gang, incomprehensible. We were kept so long whilst he checked on the trailer brakes, tare weight, and axle weights, that despite the Burrell's damper being shut down, she began to blow off. This meant of course the pencil was licked again and a further note made to the effect—" also allowing steam to blow off, on the highway."

At last we were permitted to go on our way, making a wonder-

39

ful turn of speed to make up for the time lost in Petersfield. By the time we reached Bishops Waltham it was lighting up time, the oil side lamps on the engine and the trailer tail lamp were lighted, and we were on our way again, stopping at a pub in Botley to enquire our way. Somehow in the maze of roads thereabout, we got hopelessly lost. Eventually at 1.30 a.m., we found ourselves in a very narrow road with our further progress stopped by a heavy ornamental white gate.

" Wonder where the devil we are ? " asked Cyril of Cocky Strudwick, his mate. " Up somebody's —— drive by the look of it, " replied Cocky.

" There's a house over there " chipped in Bill Standen, one of the sawing gang. " Shall I go over an' knock 'em up ? " he enquired of Cyril, and without waiting for a reply he was on his way to the house.

Seconds later there was an awful clanging followed by a string of muffled curses. The night being as black as the ace of spades, Bill had gone headlong over a half-open iron gate. Picking himself up, rubbing his leg and still cursing volubly, he struck a match and by its light he was able to find his way to the door of the house. He was about to give a knock when the door suddenly burst open and out rushed a tramp. " Hey, " shouted Bill, " don't run away, I only wanted to ask where we were."

The tramp, realising we were not the police, turned and came slowly back. " Oh yes," said he. " You are at the side drive gate of Hook Park." " Well I'll be damned," was all Bill could say in reply.

" What on earth were you doing in the house ? " asked Cyril of the tramp. " Dear me," he said in answer, " I've been sleeping here every night for over a week. The place is empty, you know, except for one room that is full of clean trusses of straw—if you are in need of accommodation for the night, I would indeed be honoured if you would accept my hospitality."

The tramp led the way in and the seven of us followed him. By the light of the candle stuck on a tin lid we viewed our abode for the night, " Well," said Cyril after some thought, " It'll be better than sleeping in the trailer." To which all readily agreed. Without further ado trusses of straw were brought in and beds were made. Meanwhile the tramp had kindled a fire in the grate and placed upon it a large tin can of water to boil. " I think I can manage tea for you all, if you have no objections to drinking it in silver cups."

Above: The Marshall 6 h.p. single cylinder portable engine and the Burrell saw-bench, the family firm's first sawmill, at work on the Leconfield Estate in 1902. The bearded figure is Harry Puddick (see pp. 21-23). **Below:** The new Clayton & Shuttleworth 6 h.p. traction on Carter Bros. stand at the Royal Counties Show, Chichester, 1908. (See pp. 27-28).

Above: The Clayton & Shuttleworth 6 h.p. single cylinder traction on road haulage in 1910. (See p. 29). **Below:** Wallis & Steveens 7 h.p. single cylinder traction hauling coal to the yard in 1917. This engine was acquired in settlement of an overdue debt. (See p. 48).

said he pointing to a row of empty condensed milk tins. He looked at me and smiled, " They're my golf and polo trophies you know."

Looking at Cyril, he said, " Actually I found myself in this area looking for a job. I suppose there is but little chance of obtaining employment with your sawmill ? " " Well," mused Cyril, " if that's all you want, you can start with our firm in the morning as a member of the mill gang." " Done," shouted the tramp, raising his tin of tea on high, " let us drink to the morrow." At this moment I suddenly became aware that his speech bore the hall-mark of a public school. As I watched him, a shadow of doubt flickered across his face as he looked down at his somewhat ragged clothes. " Dear me " he said with a sigh, " I fear my wardrobe is hardly suited to the occasion." Cyril looked at him and smiled, " Don't let that worry you, I can let you have some money in advance."

That is how Albert Singleton " the tramp " came into our employ, working with us for many years. He was tall, grey haired, a gentleman in every way, and a more talented pianist and organist I have seldom been privileged to hear. Through all the years he worked for us I cannot recall him ever being written to, or visited by any of his people, and never once did he mention to me, or my family, anything of his past life, or what made him take to life as a tramp. He remained a mystery till the day he died.

The popularity of our Burrell tractor had attracted the attention of a firm of furniture removers in a nearby town, who used a three-ton Tasker tractor for the hauling of their pantechnicon. When this engine went out of commission through a broken crankshaft, the firm applied to father for the hire of our tractor.

The first journey it did was from Four Elms, near Edenbridge. This run proved so successful that the firm of removers entered into an agreement with father for the hire of our Burrell on a three-monthly basis, father to supply the engine and driver, and they the furniture van and two packers.

Furniture " bumping " can have its trying moments like any other job. One memorable occasion, as related to me by my brother Cyril, who was driving the tractor at the time, was of a journey from Horsham to Eastbourne. Having loaded the van at Horsham they set off for Eastbourne. Arriving there late in the evening, and finding the house locked up, all three of them decided to sleep in the furniture van and unload in the morning. Just before midday, as the last of the household effects had been carried into the house, the owner

41

of the furniture, a brewer of home-made wine, produced a gallon jar of well matured rhubarb wine, and gave a tumbler full to each of them.

Cyril, realising it's potency, respectfully declined a second glass, whilst the two packers, blissfully ignorant of its potentiality, drank deep and often, with disastrous results. Both falling asleep in the van on the homeward journey, they left Cyril to cope with everything on his own.

As Cyril stopped to pick up water for the engine, one of the packers awoke with the most alarming pains in his stomach, caused, I have no doubt, by the rhubarb wine. The desperate urgency of the situation made him hurriedly alight from the tailboard of the van, and climb over the nearby hedge in search of a secluded spot, Cyril laughing merrily at the fellow's attempt to get over the hedge, and offering timely advice.

The communication cord on this occasion ran from the tailboard of the van to a large gong fitted in the cab of the engine, just above Cyril's head. Since it is imposssible for the driver to see what is going on at the back of the van from his position on the engine, it was customary when all were safely on board to give one pull on the cord to signal that all was well.

The tanks of the engine now being full, Cyril regained his driving position and waited for the all-clear on the gong. Now the hell of it all was, the whole procedure of picking up water had been watched by a group of small boys, who now that the operation was over, noticed the communication cord running along the side of the van. Wondering what it was, they gave it a pull. CLANG, went the gong, and Cyril, taking this to be the all's-well, opened the regulator of the engine and pulled away leaving the poor unfortunate packer still over the hedge.

Some considerable time later the other packer, who had been asleep all the time, woke up. On finding himself alone in the van he grabbed the cord and gave frantic signals on the gong for Cyril to stop.

" What's the trouble ? " asked Cyril, as he reached the back of the van.

" My mate. 'e aint 'ere." answered the still half-doped packer. " We must 'ave gawn an' left 'im be'ind."

" Oh my stars " Cyril ejaculated, " that was ten miles back." Then after a few moments thought he continued " Well, it's no

42

earthly good waiting for him, or we'll be here all night—he'll just have to get home the best way he can."

Having said that he turned back to the engine, climbed aboard and drove her at Hell's bat for home.

It was learned later that the unfortunate packer on hearing Cyril pull away resigned himself to his fate, and slept off the effect of the wine under the hedge. Waking in the later afternoon feeling a lot better, but still in a sad and sorry state, he walked nearly five miles to the nearest railway station, eventually reaching his home by train.

With the Burrell being on removal work so frequently it put other jobs well behind schedule, so much in fact that father had to buy another tractor quickly. Hearing of one for sale in Reading he took Bob Hooker with him to see it.

It was a 5 ton Clayton and Shuttleworth two-speed tractor with belly tanks and a full length cab, 13 months old, in perfect condition, and passed Bob's critical inspection with flying colours. Father bought her on the spot, Jacko Mills and Joe Barnett bringing her home two days later. She was a fine engine, not very fast, but exceedingly powerful, but more about her and her alarming peculiarities in a later story.

6

'Tain't honey and roses
all the way

" If 'tis anything I hate, Guv'nor " said old Joe Barnett to me, " 'tis washing out a boiler on a cold Sunday morning," and putting a grimy finger to his cheek, he squirted a vicious stream of tobacco juice at a three-quarter-inch spanner lying on the ground. There followed an outburst of language which could well have shocked a London bargee.

At this unfortunate moment my father came within earshot. " Joe," said he, " that's no language to use in the boy's hearing." The boy of course being me. I had only a few weeks previously left school, and was acting as general factotum to everyone in the yard, until the time came for me to leave home to serve my apprenticeship with another firm as a steam engineer.

" I reckon as 'ow he'll hear a lot wuss than that afore he's much older, Boss, " said Joe. And, thinking back, how right he was !

At the time of which I write, things had got into a mess in our threshing world. The six horse-power single cylinder Clayton traction had developed tube trouble, and had been brought back to the yard for re-tubing. Thus it came to be that the Burrell five-ton tractor was taken off road work, and brought into the yard for her governors to be fitted, in readiness to take over threshing duties while the Clayton was out of commission.

Old Joe had been washing out the boiler of the Burrell tractor that Sunday morning in question, and having done so, had replaced

44

all mud doors, filled the boiler with water, and screwed down the filler plate at the top of the steam chest. A bundle of firewood was placed in the tender and general preparations were made for my brother Cyril, the driver, to be away first thing on Monday morning.

My father meanwhile had detailed me to go as mate to my brother, and to take over the engine when threshing, whilst he attended to the sacks of corn coming off the threshing machine. Old Joe was to go ahead of us in the morning, to the farm where the thresher stood, to prepare everything for our arrival, and to act as feeder.

At six-thirty on Monday morning, I was at the yard, and had the fire going in the Burrell, Cyril arriving a few minutes later. Father of course, being a very strict timekeeper, was always first in the yard, and woe betide employee, or son, if late for work, and I remember now Cyril being torn off a frightful strip by father for being five minutes late.

It was an awful morning. Real November weather, with a slight fog and a touch of hoar frost, and of course still dark at that hour.

Soon after 7.30 the Burrell was lightly blowing off, and Cyril stood on the belly tank filling the mechanical lubricator. My father and I stood close behind him, waiting for him to finish oiling-up, when father noticed a wisp of steam coming from under the filler plate. " Pull those nuts down " said father to Cyril, " or you won't see for steam."

" Yes," said Cyril, and picking up a ⅝ inch spanner, he climbed back on to the tank and gave a pull at one nut. Alas, the stud broke, and all hell was let loose in a split second, all two hundred pounds per-square-inch of it.

With a deafening roar as if all the lost souls in purgatory had gone mad, the escaping steam hit Cyril fully amidships, blowing him clean off the tank, to fall to the ground, taking my father and me with him. It was pandemonium in top gear.

The roar of escaping steam made it imposssible to hear anything and the expanding steam in a cold atmosphere made it impossible to see anything. This, coupled with the fact that all three of us had been knocked to the ground, had destroyed all sense of direction. It became all too apparent to me that only by a miracle could any of us ever hope to find the engine again.

Vaguely I remember walking round in ever-widening circles

45

trying to locate her, and when at last I did, I found father there already. Somehow in the racket and roar he had got the injectors on, and was going like the clappers of hell with the clinker shovel withdrawing the fire.

I stood and gazed in spellbound bewilderment, seeing father madly shovelling, surrounded by fire, smoke, and steam. Somehow it conjured up in my mind a picture of Dante's Inferno. Dazed as I was, though, I had more respect for my young hide than to say so to father.

After what seemed an eternity the roar of steam ceased. We were then able to remove the filler plate, and renew the broken stud. A new joint was made, the boiler topped up with water, and the fire re-lighted.

By now it was well past midday, and by the time steam was raised again it was nearly two o'clock. But father insisted that we went on to the farm, and " set to " the machine, ready for next day's threshing.

Fortunately the job was only four miles away, the farm itself lying about half-a-mile off the main road. The usual type of farm approach of those days. Just a mud track, which meant spud or paddle " drill " the whole of the way from the road.

To add to our misery it started to snow. By the time we had reached the machine it was a raging blizzard.

The farmer of course had long since given us up, and had dispersed the threshing gang, leaving only old Joe, Cyril and myself to get everything ready for the next day. By the time all was done it was nearly five o'clock, and quite dark, except for the ghostly outline of everything in the snow.

With snow still falling, the prospect of a four mile walk home was not a pleasant one. But Cyril, always the optimist, said, " You follow me. I know a short cut," and proceeded to lead us out of the stack yard across the fields.

In silence we trudged through the snow, our hats pulled well down, our coat collars up to keep out the biting wind. Suddenly old Joe stopped. " Where the 'ell's Cyril gone ? " he said. He gripped my arm, and we both turned to listen.

Then came a cry for help mixed with a long string of cuss words. " Where the 'ell be you got to ? " asked Joe.

" Down here, you —— old fool," shouted Cyril.

Joe and I walked in the direction of the sound, and upon

46

looking down, we saw just his head and shoulders protruding from a small dark patch in the snow.

Joe and I grabbed him under the arms and pulled him out. The stench that came up with him was simply appalling. He had most unfortunately fallen through the rotten boards, hidden by snow, that covered the farm cesspool.

The remainder of the walk home was a veritable nightmare, with the bitter wind, snow, and the pungent aroma of distilled essence of farmyard " Chanel No. 5." Even to walk on the windward side of Cyril made it almost impossible to breathe, making one literally gasp for clean air.

As we neared our house, I was sent on ahead to warn mother of the impending pillar of stench that was about to decend upon our Home Sweet Home.

At this point perhaps it would be far better to leave my readers to imagine my mother's horror when Cyril entered the house, and also with this thought : Whatever profession you happen to follow— 'Taint Honey and Roses all the way, is it ?

7

A 7 h.p. Wallis and Steevens
comes home

EVERYONE, sooner or later, meets with a bad debt, and father was no exception to the rule. Early in 1914 he was caught rather badly through an unpaid account for sawmilling on a large farm near Chiddingfold. The debt was one the farmer could not meet, and he being the owner of a threshing set, father agreed to take it in lieu of payment of the debt with a cash adjustment. The set comprised a 7 h.p. single cylinder Wallis & Steevens traction engine, a Garrett 4 foot 6 inch threshing machine, a Massey-Harris trusser, a " Unique " elevator, and a living van.

Still working in the yard whilst waiting to begin my apprenticeship, I was ordered by father to act as steersman to " Jacko " Mills, one of our drivers, to help bring the set home.

At 6 o'clock in the morning, Jacko, George Balchin and I, left the yard on bicycles for Chiddingfold on a March morning, a morning when the Clerk of the weather must have been on holiday and forgotten to tell his second-in-command when to turn the draught fan and the water tap off, for the wind and rain were torrential. Long before reaching the farm, all three of us were soaked to the skin.

After repeated attempts with damp matches, Jacko was at long last able to get a fire going in the Wallis. With everything being so wet, more smoke came out of the fire-hole door than out of the chimney. " To hell with this," said he, " I'll warm the old —— up." Then taking a large bundle of cotton waste he poured about a pint

48

of paraffin on to it, and opening the smokebox door he put the bundle of waste in the smokebox. Unable to light a match because of the wind and rain he wound a piece of oil-soaked rag round a stick and got a light from the fire-box. Still cursing the weather he carried the spluttering torch to the front of the engine. During the interim of getting a flaming torch, the heat of the smokebox had partially vaporised the paraffin in the bundle of waste, and as he opened the smokebox door and thrust in the lighted torch, there was an almighty WHOOSH ! Flames and soot flew everywhere.

Jacko, who sported a full beard, staggered back minus the greater part of it and his eyebrows, his face the colour of a coal sack with soot. For a few seconds he stood speechless, gripping his chin with both hands. Then followed an outburst of cusswords that he must surely have learned from Satan's dictionary. It was truly terrific.

Recovering from the first shock of the explosion he picked up the lubricating oil can, and pouring a quantity of oil into one hand, he rubbed it all over his face to ease the burning. So he said. The oil mixing with the soot as he rubbed made the transformation of his features complete. He looked like one of the Devil's stokers on leave from hell.

After what seemed an eternity sufficient steam was at last raised to enable the engine to be moved, to couple up the long train of threshing tackle, pull on to the road, and head for home.

As we rundled into Chiddingfold, Jacko signalled me to steer to the side of the road, opposite a pub. " Boy " he said to me as we stopped " I need a drink mighty bad—you gwain t'ave one ? " " No thanks," I replied, " I'll stay here and look after the fire and water in the boiler." With the rain still pelting down, I was only too thankful to huddle down in the tender to absorb all the heat I could from the engine.

As Jacko and George Balchin, our guard at the end of the train, entered the public bar door, the barmaid looked up, caught sight of Jacko's oily black face, gave a frightened yell and fled ; presumably to inform the landlord, for when he returned behind the counter and saw the bedraggled pair he refused to serve them. Jacko must have told his story well, for later the landlord relented, and served them both, Jacko having a pint of strong old ale, and a half quartern of gin. Quaffing the lot in one long gulp, he returned to the engine immediately after, dabbing his burnt lips with a piece of cotton waste. " I feels a lot better now boy " he said to me as he mounted the footplate, " We'll walk this o'd iron kettle 'ome in next to no time."

" There's one thing we've forgotten, Jacko," said I.

" What's that boy ? " he enquired.

" The communication cord."

" Oh my stars, yes," said he, " Good job you reminded me, or we might 'ave got pinched," He rummaged in his tool sack to fish out a long length of stout cord, one end of which he tied to my left arm, and threaded the rest of the cord through various fittings the whole length of the train to where George, the guard, was riding.

The object of the communication cord was to enable the guard to warn the steersman, by giving one tug on the cord, to pull to the side of the road to let faster moving traffic overtake us; a series of tugs meant something was wrong, and to stop immediately.

For a mile or so all went well, until we had to negotiate a sharp bend to the right, when as we turned into the bend the communication cord grew tighter and tighter until it pulled my left arm from the steering-wheel, eventually pulling me off the steering seat. Fortunately, Jacko saw what was happening and pulled up as I fell to the ground, or I would surely have been under the wheels of the threshing machine coupled behind us. As it was, all I suffered was a large piece of skin removed from my elbow as I hit the road. What had happened was that George, the guard, had tied his end of the cord to the trusser on which he was riding, and had not allowed enough slack in the cord to negotiate a right-hand bend in the road.

This fault was soon remedied and we were on our way again. The old Wallis engine was a brute that day, owing to poor coal and the dreadful wind, she simply would not steam. Jacko tried coaxing and cursing alternately, as frequent stops were made to gain enough steam to use the injector to get more water into the boiler. The boiler feed pump had flatly refused to work from the very start of our journey, owing, it was found later, to an air leak in the suction pipe.

As darkness approached, I breathed a sigh of relief when we turned into a by-road for the last three mile lap of the journey home. Alas, all too soon, for less than a half mile ahead was an extremely short left-hand hairpin bend. Although I had steered the engine to the verge of the right-hand side of the road, to allow the train to follow round the bend, frantic tugging on the communication cord told me the manoeuvre had not worked. I reached out and touched Jacko's arm, and he snapped the regulator shut, sensing the trouble almost as soon as I touched him. Seconds later George, the guard, came running up shouting " The —— elevator's in the ditch, and the trusser's nigh in too."

Taking the communication cord from my arm and hanging it on the steering wheel, I followed Jacko back to the end of the train to see how bad the situation really was. At this moment the clerk of the weather had his finest hour of the day—the rain was simply terrific.

" This is about all we wanted," said Jacko ruefully, pushing his wet cap to the back of his head, " Dark, no lamps, rainin' like perishin' 'ell, and the —— elevator in the ditch."

" 'old 'ard a minute," said George. " There's sombudy comin' down the road on a bike."

" An' you can bet yer life it's a —— copper," said Jacko, looking in the direction of the oncoming light. " That's all we want now to finish the day."

To our great relief it was father with two white and two red hurricane lamps dangling from the handlebars of his bicycle. Knowing we had no lamps, he had come out to meet us. " What's the trouble " he enquired as he came up to where we were standing. Dejectedly Jacko explained what had happened.

By the light of the hurricane lamp, although the ditch was full of water, we were able to see that the cast-iron wheel of the elevator had broken under the strain of crashing to the bottom of the ditch.

" Ah well " said father, " There's nothing we can do about that to night—she'll have to stay there till the morning." Turning to Jacko he continued: " Uncouple her from the van Jacko, and we'll leave her for the night."

After the elevator was taken off, and the trusser brought up to the van and made fast, father placed a red lantern at each end of the derelict, then turning to me he said " You'd better get your bike from off the trusser boy and ride on home—there's a hot meal and a warm bed waiting for you there; I'll steer for Jacko the rest of the way."

With water squelching out of my boots, and the seat of my pants, fed up, cold and hungry I mounted my bicycle and rode off. I cannot remember ever being so pleased to leave an engine in all my life as I was that dreadful night. The irony of it was, the next day was sunny and warm.

8

Father meets the internal combustion engine

UP TO the year 1913 father clung desperately to his faithful friend, the horse and dog-cart, as his personal means of transport; although his business instincts told him it was fast becoming outmoded, he still continued to use the horse for journeys up to fifteen miles, and a bicycle for shorter distances.

Since our sawmills were now moving into far wider fields of operation, covering Surrey, Sussex, Hampshire and Kent, his periodical visits to the mills had to be made by train. This form of transport proved at times to be most inconvenient, as frequently he missed his connecting train and would be forced to stay in an hotel. This was something he really loathed. " I just cannot sleep in a strange bed " he would say to mother.

I have the feeling that it was not the strange bed, or his having to stay away from home for one night that worried him. Far rather would I believe it was his inability to be in the yard in the morning to see that everyone was on the job.

These circumstances forced him gradually to think in terms of buying a car. This thought was carefully nurtured by mother, whose gentle persuasion behind the scenes finally pushed him over the brink, and before he had time to reflect upon his rashness, he had become the owner of a second-hand 1910 Singer open tourer, two seater car, fitted with all the latest and up to date equipment, such as a large dickie seat at the back, canvas hood, oil burning side and tail lamps, one large acetylene gas head lamp, a long brass bulb-horn, and a " Stepney " spare rim and tyre.

When the garage proprietor from whom father had bought this wonderful piece of mechanism, delivered it to our house, excitement ran amok in the whole household. Even our maid of all work was given time off to see it. Everyone walked round admiring it, each with their own individual thoughts. Father, with a mixture of self-importance, apprehension and alarm, mother with a great amount of pride, my sister viewing it as a new definite status symbol, whilst my brother Cyril and myself, since the confounded contraption was driven by petrol, had no comment to make (no audible one that is).

" It looks very nice " said father to my mother, still walking round the car with his thumbs tucked in his waistcoat pockets, " But I haven't the remotest idea of how it works, or yet how to drive it."

" Don't fuss so, dear " answered mother, putting her arm in his and trying to instil confidence into him. " Your engineer, Bob Hooker, knows all about cars, he will teach you how to drive it very quickly."

A day or so later, when father had plucked up enough courage to have a go, Bob took the car into a large meadow at the back of our works, where, getting father seated behind the wheel, he explained what all the bits and pieces and gadgets were for. It took Bob two or three days to get him used to handling the car, and it took father several days to feel competent enough to take the car on to the road.

When at last that memorable day came, after many attempts to get the car out of the yard, father at last got it to the front door of the house. Whereupon mother was invited to take the seat at his side. This she readily did, fully dressed for the occasion complete with motoring veil in the fashion of the day.

As yet he had not grasped the idea of letting the clutch in easily when starting off, revving the engine almost to bursting point he simply took his foot off the the clutch pedal, which resulted in the car taking a flying leap into the air, dislodging mother's hat to a rakish angle, and nearly catapulting her into the dickie seat behind. His effort to change gear could be heard half a mile away.

After a few weeks of driving and hard concentration he began to get the idea of how to let the clutch in slowly, when starting off, but he never learned the art of changing gears without crashing them.

Actually, the old Singer went well, the only thing that was wrong with her was an incurable disease, that of sticking exhaust valves, resulting in periodical ear-splitting explosions in the exhaust pipe. At first these dreadful detonations alarmed father, especially on one occasion when in the High Street of Cranleigh, the old Singer let out an extra violent report, startling a horse harnessed to a baker's cart, so much that it bolted, leaving a trail of bread, cakes, etc., in its wake. However, father soon learned to accept these things as part of the joy of motoring.

A month or so after buying the car, he was returning home from a visit to Baynards Station one day and had reached a point about a quarter of a mile from the yard when the old car really excelled herself by letting go the king of all explosions in the exhaust, blowing the silencer into a thousand bits, and setting fire to the floor under the dickie seat. Father was blissfully unaware of this until he got out of the car after pulling into the yard.

Seeing the flames and smoke coming from the open dickie, he shouted at the top of his voice. " Fire, Bob, Fire ! " Whereupon Bob came running from the fitting shop with a pail of water and threw the lot including the pail into the dickie to quench the flames. This catastrophe so unnerved father that a few days later he had sold the car, and returned to a more leisurely and dignified mode of transport, his horse or his bicycle.

At about this time I had started my apprenticeship with the firm of engineers at Wisborough Green, some six miles away. For the purpose of getting to and from work I had purchased a 1911 Douglas 2¾ h.p. flat-twin belt drive motor cycle, the type with the engine mounted high up under the petrol tank, and a large diameter flywheel.

Having been asked to play cricket for our local team and being one of the elite of the village (in my own estimation, of course), I therefore dressed in full white cricket regalia. Being a little late, but more to show off the Douglas than any other reason, I decided to go to the match on my motorbike.

All was going well until I reached the centre of Alfold village. Here, of all places, my thin, white, trouser leg fluttering in the wind caught up in the castellated nut of the whirring flywheel, winding itself round until it ripped the trouser leg completely off, nearly throwing me over the handlebars as the engine stopped under the extra load.

There on the side of the road I suffered the indignity, to say nothing of the damage to my ego, of having to disentangle what remained of my trouser leg from the flywheel, with the greater part of my underwear in full view of the passer by, including one whom I would have given the world not to have seen in this sorry plight —my ex-girlfriend.

Blazing with fury, I decided there and then that the Douglas must go. A week later I had part-exchanged her for a 1912 3½ h.p. Triumph belt drive with a Sturmey Archer 3-speed hub.

Talking to father one Saturday afternoon, I enquired of him " Now that you are without a car, why don't you try to ride a motor-bike ? " Fully expecting a rude answer, I was astonished to hear him say " Now that really is a good idea—can I try on yours ? "

With some misgiving I brought the Triumph on to the road, and carefully explained to him what he had to do to get started. " Set the air and throttle levers thus, lift the exhaust lever, run by the side of the bike until she fires, then hop into the saddle."

" That all sounds simple enough," said father, taking the handlebars. " I think I can manage that alright." Then running like a hare beside the bike he let go the exhaust, and as the engine fired he took a flying leap for the saddle with the agility of an acrobat. Unfortunately he jumped right over it, to spread-eagle himself, face downwards, on the road, while the Triumph careered on into the ditch.

I must say he looked a sorry mess as he picked himself up from where he lay on the road. Huge chunks of skin missing from his nose, hands, chin and knees, with blood everywhere. His capabilities in the use of expletives were always of a very high standard, but what he had to say about motor bikes on that occasion would fill a large book if only one dared to publish it.

A day or so after father's attempt to ride a motorcycle, as he was sitting in a deck chair on the lawn nursing the wounds received from that escapade and talking to my brother Cyril about the next day's work, Cyril casually remarked, " Oh by the way, I hear that Sir George so-and so is selling his Stanley Steam Car. Now that should really suit you, with no gears to change." " Umm," said father thoughtfully, " I know as much about them as I do the other sort." Eventually Cyril's arguments in favour of a steam car won him over.

The following day they both went to see the Stanley, and after

Above: The only car Father ever drove successfully—a 1914 Model T Ford, (see pp. 53-57). **Below:** The Clayton & Shuttleworth 5-ton tractor, (No. 45998), that killed " Fairy " Amery (see p. 74) and was involved in so many inexplicable accidents.

Above: The 6 h.p. single cylinder Burrell which replaced the fateful Clayton in 1918 (see p. 74). With the maker's number 1596, she was completed on 26th March, 1892. Below: The Aveling & Porter tandem roller is at last loaded onto a train at Kingston station. (See p. 79).

a trial run, with Sir George's man driving, father decided on the spot to purchase it, and proudly, Cyril drove it home. Incidentally, he and I were the only two on the firm who ever did drive it.

As I have already told you, father's mechanical knowledge was absolutely nil, and though he was given a great number of lessons on how to ignite the oil burner, each time he tried to do it on his own the whole car became enveloped in flames. He would then rush out of the shed where the Stanley stood, yelling hell fire and blue murder for Bob, or anyone else in the vicinity, to come and put it out. If I remember correctly, the Stanley's life with us amounted to exactly four weeks and two days before sharing the same fate as the Singer.

My brother and I were truly disgusted with him for selling her for she really was a beautiful machine, powerful, silent as the night, and elegant.

By this time father's need of transport was acutely desperate; finally he placed an order for a new 1914 Model T Ford, which was delivered to him direct from Manchester a short while before war was declared on Germany in the August of that year.

The old " Tin Lizzie " was the only car he was ever able to drive with any measure of success. I can see him now, if going in the direction of the school in the morning, stopping to pick up all the children he could cram into the car, then dropping them at the school door. If he didn't have a car full of children, it would be full of dogs. How they all loved him, dogs and kiddies alike.

You asked, " What happened to the horse ? " Well— father loved his horse far too much ever to sell her, she was given the freedom of the meadow and stable, to roam just as she so pleased.

9

Life at one of our sawmills

THE DECLARATION of war in 1914, of course, temporarily put paid to all except the most urgent furniture removals, as every engine we possessed went on to war contracts. The five sets of sawmills ceased their estate work, and turned to producing timber for military use. Father's entire staff, now numbering one hundred and twenty two, were all exempt from military service, including the two engineers, carpenter, painter and blacksmith, who worked in the yard.

War work seemed to bring to light many hidden talents in some of our employees who often found themselves doing a kind of work that even they never thought they would be asked to do. Joe Barnett was one of these. Joe had been in our employ twelve years or more as a general handyman and was now a member of a sawing gang on a war contract in a large forest near Bentley in Hampshire, as a timber cross-cutter. It was here that he astounded father by his remarkable ability to sharpen a circular saw. He was so delighted with his discovery, that Joe was promoted to sawyer, and was placed under Jack Whittington, the head sawyer, to learn the art.

Two months later, Joe found himself installed as second sawyer on one of our three bench mills working at Pendeen Forest near Midhurst.

Joe's prowess with an axe too was well known among our sawing gangs. He could swing a 7 lbs. timber felling axe with the best of them. This led to some friendly rivalry with the timber fellers, and frequent bouts were arranged between them and the sawing gang, to see who could cut through a nine inch log in the least number of strokes. Each put sixpence in the pool, and the winner took the lot, the winnings usually being spent in the village pub in the evening.

Before any of these bouts took place, Joe would get to work on his axe and hone the edge of it till it was as sharp as a razor. Indeed I have seen him test the edge of his axe by licking the back of his arm and literally shaving the hair from it.

Almost every night in the week you would find the greater part of the sawing gang in the taproom of the local pub, and if the timber fellers should come in, there was always plenty of horse-play and banter between the rival gangs. One night in particular an argument arose as to who could strike with the greatest accuracy with an axe. It was agreed that on the following night the contestants should bring their own axes to the pub, the contest to be fought out in the taproom, with George Singleton, the mill engineer and driver appointed as umpire and holder of the stakes.

On the night in question, George arrived at the pub with a large block of hard wood with several holes drilled in the end that were just big enough to take a matchstick. The block was then placed on the flag-stone floor of the taproom and one matchstick was placed in an upright position in one of the holes.

Three rules were stipulated : one, that no preliminary aim was allowed; two, the axe must be swung from the shoulder; three, the matchstick must be split from top to bottom right down through the centre, with one blow of the axe.

When the landlord of the pub finally became aware of what was to take place in his taproom that night, he almost fainted. Vainly he pleaded with them to stop it, but the only reply he got was, if he didn't shut up they would put him on the block instead of the matchstick.

The taproom was full to overflowing that night with the rival gangs, and with local lads who came to see the fun. After the rules had been agreed to, and several pints had been consumed, the contest started in earnest. Soon the number of those taking part was reduced to two, Joe Burnett for the sawing gang, and Bill White for the timber fellers, as matchstick for matchstick they kept even with each other.

The excitement was intense, but the winner was never proved. Why ? Well ! One of the local lads, who was well known as a practical joker, borrowed the game-keeper's twelve bore gun, then going to the taproom door he quietly opened it, pointed the gun into the air and watched through the chink of the door. When he saw the axe, which happened to be Joe's start to descend he pulled the trigger. The almighty bang that followed so startled Joe that he not only missed the matchstick, but missed the block as well. The axe hit the flag-stone floor with a crash, with disastrous results to the razor-like edge.

In a towering rage Joe dropped his axe to the floor swearing bloody murder upon the culprit. As he lurched toward the taproom door, bent on revenge, two of the timber felling chaps put out their hands to restrain him. Joe, seeing red, lashed out at them right and left, and in seconds the taproom was a bedlam of flying fists in a " Free for All " as pint mugs, and beer, went scattering over the saw-dust covered floor.

Mercifully, it was all stopped as quickly as it had begun by the landlord's daughter, who jumped up on to a heavy wooden table, that stood by the serving hatch of the cellar door, and blasted out the " Gone Away " on a hunting horn. So astonished was everyone by the piercing sound of the horn, that the fighting ceased immedi-ately. Having thus gained their attention, she told them in no un-certain way, that they were all damned fools and the only decent thing to do was to spend the stake money in beer, enough for three gallons, and drink all round as friends.

Timber feller and sawyer alike acclaimed this a wonderful idea, and as they drank together peace reigned once more in the taproom of the Old Oak Tree Inn.

Who fired the gamekeeper's shotgun that night ? Well ! Most of our sawing gang tried to find the answer to that question, and not the least of them was Joe, but it remained a carefully guarded secret in Pendeen. It is well that it did, or the fight would have started all over again.

It was customary during the war for our sawmills to work through the Saturday and Sunday of every alternate week-end, and on a great many occasions I would be granted leave of absence from the firm to whom I was apprenticed, on Saturday mornings to act as a relief driver of the engine at the Pendeen mill, to enable George Singleton, the permanent driver, to return home to his wife, who at that period was desperately ill.

When it was my turn for duty, I would arrive on a motorcycle late on Friday evening, and return to my home Sunday night, accommodation for me at the mill being arranged by father, in one of the living vans on the mill site. Each van was fitted with six bunks, in tiers of three on either side, and mine was at the top, on the opposite side to the entrance door, and heaven be praised, it was close to the window and the ventilator.

Each bunk, in all the vans, was supplied with its own flock mattress and blankets but I suspect mother had a hand in the arrangements for mine, for I had sheets, pillow and slip, a luxury the other inmates seemed not to worry about. They preferred to sleep mostly in their clothes, merely removing their boots and cap. Sometimes, after a particularly hectic night at the Old Oak Tree Inn, they would even disregard this formality.

On such occasions as this I would thank my guardian angel for giving me the bunk near the window, for the stench that arose in such a confined space, can be better imagined than described.

At my first and subsequent visits to the Pendeen mill father placed me under the care of old Joe, not that he was better than any of the others, but father knew that as far as Joe was concerned there would never be a shortage of food, for though it was war time and rationing was in force, Joe knew his way about far too well to be short of a meal.

On my first spell of relief duty at the mill, I arrived tired and hungry on the Friday night, then after making my bed in the top bunk, I walked out of the van to where Joe was standing stirring the red-hot embers of the camp-fire with a long stick.

" What have we got for supper tonight, Joe ? "

" Ah! young guv'ner," replied Joe, "We got summat special."

" Oh, and what's that ? "

" Bre'n butter, baked swede, baked 'taters, an' roasted 'edge 'og." smiled Joe in answer.

" Roast hedge-hog ? " I repeated incredulously. " You're pulling my leg."

" No I ain't," said Joe, " Get your plate an' eatin' tools, 'cause 'tis all ready t'eat."

Still unbelieving, I stood and watched him as he deftly removed from the hot embers, four huge potatoes, a large swede, and finally a big ball of clay, which he rolled on to a flat stone, and gently tapped round its equator, as it were, with a stick. When a crack appeared all round the ball of clay, Joe gingerly lifted off the top part,

Joe cooks a hedgehog for the evening meal. (*Drawing by Miss A. Child*).

revealing the contents. It really *was* a hedge-hog, the skin and the spines coming away with the clay.

At the sight of it my stomach did a somersault in revolt, and I stepped back, feeling as sick as a dog.

" What's up ? " enquired Joe, noticing my pallor.

" My god, Joe," I managed to jerk out, " I can't eat that." Though I must admit in all fairness it smelt damn good.

" Well ! If you can't I can." said he, tucking in to his share with apparent relish, " So I rec'on you'll 'ave to make do wid bre'n cheese. Though tomorrer," he continued between large mouthfuls, " I'll cook 'e a chicken an' swede pie."

When the mill had stopped for lunch the following day, Joe hurriedly ate his cold sausages, and set to work to prepare our evening meal. Selecting two medium sized swedes, he cut off the top of each about a third of the way down, then scooping out a hole in the middle, he put in a big lump of pork dripping, a small onion, salt, and pieces of chicken. The tops of the swedes were then replaced and fastened down with thin slivers of wood, all items being placed in an upright position in the ashes of the camp-fire, and covered with the hot embers.

" Ah ! That be that," sighed Joe, walking back to where I was standing and wiping the blade of his jack-knife on his trouser leg, " I reck'n that'll be fit t'eat 'bout seb'n t'night."

As Joe and I walked back with the rest of the sawing gang to the vans that evening after the mill had closed down, he looked at me with a twinkle in his eyes and asked, " You 'ungry t'night guv'ner ? "

I looked up into his smoke stained face. " I'm that hungry Joe I believe I could eat a horse."

" Good," said Joe, smiling broadly.

Upon reaching our van I got to work with soap and water, and noticed with some concern, that Bill Thayre, the head sawyer, Bert Parsons, the third sawyer, and I were the only members of our van crew who washed. The others, including Joe regarded it as a wasted effort and only did so on the weekend they were going home.

While I was engaged in my ablutions, Joe had retrieved the two swedes from the ashes and had stood them upright in two enamelled bowls.

" There y'are guv'ner," said he, blowing away the ashes and removing the tops of the swedes, " You git stuck inter that."

The aroma that wafted across my nostrils made my stomach gurgle with delightful anticipation, and to use Joe's expression, I really got " stuck inter it," even to scraping the inside of the swede almost clean with my spoon, while Joe watched me with a grin of satisfaction and amusement."

On the Sunday night as I was about to leave the mill for home, Joe came to see me off. " So you liked your chicken pie, Guv'ner, did 'ee ? " he enquired, laughing, and putting another quid of tobacco into his mouth.

" Oh yes Joe I did indeed, and thank you very much."

Joe laughed heartily. " I'm glad 'bout that," he said, I looked at him quizzically. Then he continued, " 'cos that was your share of th' 'edge 'og."

I wanted to be sick, but what was the use of trying to vomit up something you had eaten twenty-four hours before.

I simply cannot leave the story of the Pendeen mill, and the escapades of Joe, without telling you of how we came to have pork for several meals.

Joe it seems had made friends with a nearby farmer, for a more subtle reason than just being pals. The occasional load of firewood, mysteriously disappearing from the mill, came back to Joe, more often than not, in the form of butter and milk.

One evening Joe stood talking to the farmer by the pigsty, discussing a litter of pigs. " It's that 'en there," said the farmer pointing to the smallest one of the litter. " If I could find anyone as could kill 'en, on the quiet like, we'd 'ave 'en fer ourselves indoors."

Joe stood rubbing his chin and thinking hard for some few seconds before he spoke. " Well, I reckon I could kill an' dress 'en for 'ee. When do 'ee want 'en done ? "

" Day a'ter tomorrer, if that be alright for 'ee." answered the farmer.

" That's right 'nough for me." said Joe, then bidding the farmer good night, he turned away, and made for the Old Oak Tree Inn, very deep in thought.

Late on the night before the slaughter was to be done, Joe left the van without saying a word to anyone, taking with him a darning needle and some black powder, taken from a 12 bore cartridge. Finding his way to the pigsty in the half moonlight, he rounded up the pig that was to be killed into one corner of the sty, Then with the needle he made several small jabs with it on the pig's rump, just enough to break the skin, then rubbed in a small quantity of the black powder.

The next afternoon, when Joe arrived to kill the pig, he and the farmer stood by the sty, Joe eyeing the poor unfortunate beast with an expression of alarm on his face. " Farmer," he at last blurted out, " That there pig's got summat wrong wid 'en, looks t' me as if 'e got some sort o' fever."

" I can't see nothen wrong wid 'en," said the farmer, looking hard at the pig, " 'cept 'e ent as big as t'others."

" Ahh ! 'e got summat wrong." drawled Joe, looking very wise, " but I reckon we better kill 'en though, all ' same."

After the pig had been killed, and was in the tub of boiling water to remove the hair and top skin, Joe suddenly pointed to the pig's rump and shouted, " Look farmer, 'ere 'tis. I know'd 'e 'ad summat wrong wid 'en, 'es got spotted fever. You can't eat 'en, 't 'ould kill 'ee for sure."

" Oh my Gawd," said the unsuspecting farmer, looking hard at the black spots, " what ever be I gwain t' do wid 'en. I 'spose I'll 'ave to bury 'en in the garden."

" Lord no, you maun do that, or all t'others 'll get it," said Joe in a very grave tone.

" What th 'ell can I do wid'en then ? " asked the farmer.

" Well," answered Joe, scratching the back of his neck and appearing to think hard, " t'ould be safer for all t'others for me to take 'em back to the mill, and burn 'en in the firebox of th'old ingine."

For several days after that all the mill gang had joints of pork to eat, roast, boiled, baked and stewed. While Joe, I might add, finished up with several shillings in his pocket for beer, from the sale of pork to the rest of the mill gang, but none of them ever knew how Joe had managed to get the pig, and for that matter, they never asked.

10

The ripe old age
of seventeen

1917—AH YES ! That was the year I attained the ripe old age of seventeen years myself, and I suppose like most teenagers of then, and now, thought I knew it all.

That was the year, too, that my apprenticeship was cut short by His Majesty's Government's desire for me to render assistance to my King and country as an engineer in the Royal Navy.

What with the war, and the tremendous amount of work to be done in the haulage line, my father was having a worrying time, the shortage of men being the most pressing.

At the time of which I write, several government contracts were held by our firm for haulage. Among them was one for the haulage of pit props from Leith Hill, and Coldharbour to Ockley station, a distance of some seven to eight miles.

Owing to the untimely demise of one of our drivers, my father was able to persuade my Lords of the Admiralty to grant me a three months' deferment to fill the breach as it were—as a driver.

Thus at the tender age of seventeen I found myself in charge of a five ton Burrell tractor on the pit-prop haulage contract.

Of our own engines there was a Clayton and Shuttleworth 6 h.p. two-speed agricultural traction and a Wallis and Steevens traction, 7 h.p. two-speed, of about 1895 vintage, the one acquired by us in lieu of debt. These two engines were used solely for the haulage of trees from the " warren " to a piece of common land, where they were cut to length, graded, and loaded on to our trailers for haulage to Ockley station. There the props were unloaded from the trailers and loaded into rail wagons by another gang of men.

For the haulage side we had our own Burrell tractor, to which I was appointed driver, and on hire to us from various owners were : an Aveling and Porter 8 h.p. three-speed road locomotive, a Tasker 5 tons three-speed tractor, a Ransomes 5 ton two-speed tractor, and a Wallis and Steevens three ton two-speed tractor.

The general idea, I found, seemed that to be a *real* driver one had to consume as much beer in a day as the engine did water.

Under this ruling I was not a qualified driver, and was frequently reminded of it, jestingly, by the others, for in spite of all my seventeen years I had not as yet acquired the art of drinking. This fault, I might add, was remedied during my sea-going career.

Any of my readers knowing the Ockley-Leith Hill area of yesteryear will be well aware of the narrowness of the roads and the steepness of the hills. Because of this we were routed one way " outbound," and one way " homebound," to avoid the difficulty of passing each other.

Each engine had it's own set of trailers—one being loaded, one en route, and one being unloaded. In this way a continuous shuttle was run. With the 8 h.p. Aveling, of course, nine trailers were used, three at a time.

As an added incentive to work, each driver was paid above his weekly wage the vast amount of sixpence for each load he delivered, and the trailer brakesmen twopence.

This caused some rivalry, and if upon your return your own trailer was not ready, well ! you pinched someone else's that was, carefully avoiding those of the Aveling, as they were far too heavy for we tractor blokes.

This trailer pinching led to our first disaster. One of mine had given out, and a new one was delivered to me from Tasker's and at only a week old was pinched by the Wallis three-tonner.

Just what happened is not quite clear, but it appears that the brakeman, who rode on a little seat at the back near the brake-wheel, fell off. The driver, unaware of this, and going like the clappers of hell, lost control. He jumped clear, and left the engine and trailer to their own devices.

The little Wallis hit the bank on one side, then careered down a steep slope on the other.

Alas ! my new trailer finished up like matchwood. The

Wallis had a broken flywheel, bent crank, bent hind-wheel and front axle, the cab, chimney, chimney base and safety valves were smashed off.

My first minor mishap came during my first fortnight. The Klinger gauge glass broke. Being an odd size, and war-time, our firm was unable to get a replacement, and for six weeks I drove without a water gauge. The gods must surely have been on my side, for I never once dropped the plug.

The sixpence per load referred to was my final undoing. You see, it became the practice of the tractor drivers on the two mile slope to the main road, to throw the engines out of gear and coast, placing their entire faith in the hind-wheel brakes, the trailer brakeman, and the Devil himself.

Thus one Saturday morning on the said slope with the engine out of gear, I met my Waterloo. A six-foot by nine-inch pit prop lay in the road, evidently fallen from the load preceding me.

Hitting it with one front wheel tore the steering wheel from my hand. At some ungodly speed we careered across the grass verge, straight through a ten foot high, close-paled wooden fence that surrounded the kitchen garden of a large house, coming to rest within a few feet of the old gardener who was working a full fifteen feet from the fence. The startled look on his face is still with me in memory. And his first remark seemed to me so inadequate : " 'Ow the —— did you get in 'ere ? "

The tractor following me roped the engine and trailer back on to the road, but owing to meeting a small obstacle en route to the garden—a roadside ditch—the perch bracket had been pushed up into the smoke-box, and I was utterly out of commission.

Perhaps it would not be quite polite for me to record the exact words of my father when he discovered the real cause of the accident—coasting out of gear. But I can record with no uncertainty that I was in the Navy ten days later.

As one of our old drivers said to me a year or so back : " Them wuz 'appy days, guv'ner ! "

11

A "Jonah" comes to our yard

FOR SEVERAL months past, the Clayton and Shuttleworth tractor that father had purchased from a firm in Reading, had been giving perfect service in a great variety of jobs. Never once had she given Jacko Mills trouble of any kind. For that matter Jacko sang her praises loudly, and was proud to be her driver.

She had been engaged for a few weeks hauling bricks, timber, etc., from Milford Station to the new camp being built at Witley for the Canadian army, and now, father had recalled her to the yard to drive a rack sawbench to convert round timber into scantlings and planks for our own use.

Jacko, now that father had engaged a new driver for the Clayton tractor, reluctantly handed her over to the new man, and resumed his duty as driver of the Wallis and Steevens 7 h.p. traction engine that had now been completely re-conditioned and painted in our own works.

The new driver, Jack Amery, was a genial, quick-witted, likeable fellow, always laughing and who, by reason of his stature— 6 foot 2 inch and weighing over 12 stones—was quickly dubbed with the nickname " Fairy." He was also a strict teetotaller. This fact father could never fully comprehend, it was simply unheard of— a driver who did not take alcohol. Thus it came to be, that for the first time in the history of the firm, we had a total abstainer in our midst.

Whether this most unusual occurrence had aught to do with

the queer happenings over the next two years, or if the Clayton tractor, as one or two of the older employees of the firm thought, was bewitched, I don't know. As for father, we always knew him to be superstitious ; and though he would never admit it, he was just a little inclined toward the belief in witchcraft, as indeed were quite a number of the older fellows in our village. As for me, well, I had an open mind on the whole subject, though the peculiar behaviour of the Clayton tractor after the arrival of Fairy, gave a heck of a lot of food for thought and head wagging, especially to the older fraternity.

For a few days, after Fairy had taken over, nothing untoward happened. Then one morning as Fairy left his position on the engine to assist in rolling a large log on to the table of the rack bench, this seemed to be the moment the Clayton tractor had been waiting for, for just as they got the log halfway up, she threw off her governor belt. With a roar she was away, gaining speed at a frightening rate and prancing like a young high-spirited Arab Steed. The mill gang let go the log and dived for cover as the saw, now doing three to four times its normal speed, was throwing out sparks as it wobbled against the steel guides, and a shower of inserted teeth flew in all directions like bullets from a gun.

Father, hearing the racket, ran from his office to see what the commotion was about. " Blimey Guv'ner," said Fairy, still shaking as father reached him, " that was an anxious moment." For by now he had managed to stop the engine.

Father walked round the plant to see what damage had been done, as he did so he gave a sigh of relief, " Well ! Thank the Lord no one has been hurt, and all we seem to have lost, is a nearly new driving belt and a 5 foot circular saw."

The breaking of a governor belt is something that has happened to practically every driver in the course of his career, and there is nothing outstanding about this case, except that it was the first of a series of inexplicable, and strange coincidences.

Not more than three weeks after the story just quoted, Fairy drove into the yard one evening and pulled right round to face the main gates, ready to get away in the morning. Leaving the Clayton tractor standing quietly, he and his mate filled a few sacks with coal to put on the trailer, ready for the next day.

Suddenly, and without any warning, the regulator of the Clayton tractor flew wide open. The h.p. crank must have been on the right centre for she started up and charged straight at Fairy and his mate like a mad bull, they jumping deftly to one side as she plunged into the twenty tons of coal in the bay, climbing halfway up it before coming to a halt.

This strange incident had been witnessed by father, my brother Cyril, and one or two men in the yard. " What the hell made her do that ? " enquired father of Cyril. " I'm damned if I know," he answered, somewhat bewildered. They walked over to the tractor and examined her, and, coming to no definite conclusion, the matter was dismissed with father's final comment—" How extraordinary ! "

A few months had now elapsed since the Clayton tractor's first run-away and as no further incident had occurred the matter was more or less forgotten. Then one day as Fairy was hauling granite for the Rural District Council, from Baynards station to points along the Withybush—Cranleigh road, while he and his mate were shovelling granite from a railway truck into the trailer, the regulator blew open again. This time she careered up the station goods yard, coming to rest, with a crash, in the side of a railway goods van, staving in her smokebox door, breaking her chimney off at the cast-iron base, pushing the cab back nine inches or more, and causing quite a bit of damage to the goods van.

When the Clayton tractor was hauled back to the yard and father was given the news of this latest catastrophe, with an inventory of the damage, he, quite justifiably, flew into a violent temper and called Cyril, Bob Hooker, and me (at that time I was home on leave, from the sea), into his office for an engineering consultation. " Look" said he, in stern finality, " Something has got to be done about this —— engine before she kills someone. So get out there all three of you, and find out why the hell she does it," and to add emphasis to his last remark he crashed his fist down onto his desk with such ferocity as to send his ink-stand flying. " Blast everything," he spat out with such venom, that all three of us retreated hurriedly from his presence to the calmer atmosphere of the yard.

Bob and Cyril dismantled the regulator valve, which on this model of Clayton was of the piston type, made of cast bronze and machined to a shape rather like a cotton reel and made to slide to and fro in a cast-iron bush, with high pressure steam at either end of the valve to equalize it. All three of us examined it with meticulous care, but could find no mechanical reason for its mysterious behaviour. After a consulation with father, who by now had cooled off some-

71

what, it was agreed to replace the valve, with strict instructions that no matter who should drive her, she was never to be left, under any circumstances, without the reversing lever being placed in the neutral position, and Fairy, most of all, stuck hard and fast to this ruling.

Now, all went well for several weeks, until the November of 1917, when Fairy was hauling sawn timber from our mill working at Shillinglee Park, to Witley station. As the trailer was being loaded, Fairy, to save time, un-coupled the Clayton tractor from the trailer and backed her down to the edge of the nearby lake to fill the tanks with water before leaving for Witley. He had placed the end of the suction hose into the lake and was returning to the engine to turn on the steam for the water lift, when, believe it or not, the regulator flew open once more. As she leaped backwards into the lake the coils in the suction hose lying on the ground caught Fairy's leg and dragged him into the lake as well, nearly drowning the poor fellow.

When this news was imparted to father, his blood reached almost boiling point with temper; slamming the telephone down, he stormed round the office like a mad bull, his face taking on the colour of what I believe is known as puce.

Before the Clayton tractor had been pulled from the lake and back to the yard, Fairy was called to the office for interrogation, and the probability of the sack. Here, in father's presence, he was prepared to swear before his Maker that he had left the reversing lever in the neutral notch, and by some mysterious means it had been moved from that position to that of full reverse. That was his story, and, God bless him, he stuck to it.

" But," said father, " That's impos—" He stopped abruptly. " Unless " he continued in alarm, his mind flicking to the supernatural, " There is a poltergeist at work."

" I don't know who 'e is Guv'ner," Fairy murmured softly, " But I swear to you I never see anybody else there 'cept me."

Father, by now was too perplexed to even think clearly, and Bob, and Cyril were called to the office, and after consulting them both it was agreed that Clayton and Shuttleworth's advice should be sought on the matter.

In due course one of Clayton's representatives and an engineer called to see the engine. The engineer, on stripping the regulator valve down, came to the same conclusion that Cyril, Bob, and I had, i.e., that there was absolutely nothing wrong with it, and as a suggestion, for the small cost involved, we could try fitting a new valve and bush. This was done, and the engine returned to work, with Fairy still as her driver.

It is strange, to say the least, since many of us on the firm had driven the Clayton tractor at various times, yet these things only happened when Fairy was driving. There must have been a logical answer to it of course, but I, or Cyril and Bob, for that matter couldn't find it. Little do I wonder that father, in desperation turned to the supernatural.

Here I will leave the Clayton tractor for the moment and return to father. It was a recognised thing, that in fair weather or foul, he would always visit Guildford market every Tuesday. There he would meet all his business associates, estate owners, and representatives of various firms.

A few days after Christmas, 1917, Fairy approached father for two days off to go to London to visit his sister who was ill. " That's alright," agreed father, adding, " If you would like to make it Tuesday next, I can give you a lift in the Ford as far as Guildford to help you on your way."

Tuesday morning came, and Fairy and father left for Guildford, father returning home at his usual hour in the late afternoon in joyful mood. At ten o'clock that night he complained of aching pains, and retired to bed with a " Hot Toddy " of rum. Wednesday morning mother called in the family doctor, whose diagnosis was " 'Flu," the virulent so-called " Spanish 'Flu " then ravaging this country for the first time. On Thursday father passed out of our lives, at the age of fifty-one.

Our entire staff, now numbering 170, were for taking his body to the church on a low trailer with no sides, behind his first new traction engine, the Clayton 6 h.p. Mother, quite understandably, would not hear of this. They were however, not to be outdone and pressed for mother to dispense with the hearse, that they might carry him to his last resting. So, as his body was brought from the house, six of our stalwarts lifted his coffin to their shoulders, and bore him away towards the church. The rest of our men had stationed themselves at 50 yard intervals along the route, and as the cortege reached them, so they would change bearers, right to the altar of the church. Thus they showed their loyalty to and affection for the " Guv'ner " they all loved.

My brother Cyril, being the eldest of the family, was now appointed by mother, the sole beneficiary under father's will, as

73

general manager, and later, he and I received directorships. All credit to him, for he made a wonderful manager; but to return to the Clayton tractor and Fairy.

For several months now she had been on good behaviour. She had tried on the odd occasion to take off, but now that she had been fitted with a flywheel brake, and with Fairy, whenever he had to leave her, meticulous in his care to wind this brake on and to put the reversing lever in the neutral position, she had little chance to get away.

Fairy was now engaged in hauling round timber into our mill working at Penshurst in Kent. Having completed his loading, and securing the trees to the timber tug by chains, he moved the tractor round to couple up to the tug. Backing toward the drawbar he missed the coupling pin hole by a fraction of an inch, and jumped down from the tender of the engine to assist his mate to pull the heavy drawbar over to enable the drawpin to fall into place.

This action of Fairy's was the one the Clayton had waited so long for. For the last time the regulator flew open. Hurtling backward she pushed the drawbar to one side throwing his mate clear, but catching poor Fairy between her tender and the butt of a large tree, killing him instantly. When Cyril heard this dreadful news over the telephone he sank into his office chair, and cried like a child. After all the years, this was our first fatal accident.

No one on our firm would go to Penshurst to drive the Clayton tractor home, not even Jacko Mills, who had always thought the world of her, Eventually, she was towed back by our Wallis 7 h.p. traction engine.

After a lapse of several months, we part exchanged her for a two speed 6 h.p. single cylinder Burrell, a remarkably fine engine.

The Clayton tractor was eventually driven from our yard by her new owner, and though we were constantly in touch with him, never once did we hear that her regulator ever blew open again.

I often wondered, Why ? The old-timers wagged their heads knowingly when ever she was spoken about. We young-'uns just wondered. Call it fate, witchcraft, black-magic, or what you like, the facts still remain the same. Whether Fairy or the Clayton was the Jonah—I just don't know.

12

That road roller question

" DO YOU KNOW anything about steam rollers ? " enquired the Surveyor of our Rural District Council. " Well ! " I replied, " Apart from putting in new fireboxes, stays, tubes, plating hind and front rolls and repairs to the top motion—I don't know a lot about 'em."

We certainly didn't use them in our business, and I did not meet up with them during my sea career, but quite a few were repaired for other people in our yard at home. However, that has nothing to with this story.

Having served some time afloat, I thought I would like a change. I packed in the sea and secured an appointment with a firm of Steam Rolling Contractors in Dorset, as representative engineer (much to the disgust of Mother and Cyril at home).

A week or so was spent in their office getting the low-down on everything. Then I was turfed out to take up my duties outside ; my area of work being the Southern Counties. After a week or so of meeting surveyors, and viewing our rollers working in their areas, I one day received a letter from head office asking me to go to Ham Street, Kent, there to meet driver X, off rail from Waterloo; take him to a farm some few miles out where lay a roller, van and watercart. Arrange to load all on rail and consign to Redhill, Surrey, for work there.

I had no difficulty in picking out my man at the station—a weedy looking fellow with a sack slung over his shoulder and a greasy case tied up with binder twine in his hand; his coat and trousers so saturated with oil of several years' vintage, and so highly polished that I thought he was wearing oilskins.

" Are you Driver X ? " I enquired. " Yez'ir," said he. Then followed a speech I was utterly unable to translate and can only hope to spell phonetically.

" Ahh, an' I d'naw wat thee d' wan' I var tew. Thee d' wan. I take on thik Roller don' ee'. 'eer casn't be done 'snow. I zin 'er avoar. 'ers all done 'snow."

Not wishing to let him know that I hadn't understood a word of what he had said, I decided to ask no more questions, so bundled him into the car and drove off.

After exhaustive enquiries we eventually found the farm and the roller, an Aveling and Porter 8 ton single cylinder, of great age. My first sight of her revealed a little of the meaning of the driver's first outburst. I put her down to be about 1890 vintage and, according to the farmer, she had been lying there eleven months or more, unsheeted and unattended. What the brass and copper hunters hadn't destroyed, the winter's severe frosts had. There was nothing for it but to notify the office and consign the whole lot back to the works for scrap.

There is nothing in this part of the story that is out-standing, except a reminder to all owners to drain out everything before they lay any kind of steam engine up for the winter.

The next episode worthy of note started by the receipt of a telegram from head office to go to the firm's yard at Kingston-on-Thames. There a letter awaited me giving instructions to see a roller loaded on rail, and consign it to High Wycombe.

This turned out to be an Aveling and Porter 6 ton Tandem Roller with a vertical boiler. On this type the driving roll is in the front, under the coal bunker and water tank, the rear rolls being the steerage, The engine is a double h.p. cylinder type with no flywheel, but a heavy balanced crank fitted with radial valve gear for quick reversing. Also fitted is a steam steerage unit with three cylinders. This engine drives through a worm gear to a quadrant fitted on top of the roll fork above a large swan-neck frame. The steering is controlled by a single steerage lever at the driver's right hand, working on a plain quadrant by the side of the reverse lever. The reversing lever, of course, works on a notched quadrant in the usual mnaner. To operate the steering, the lever is pushed forward to turn left, and pulled back to turn right, in the centre position the steerage is stationary.

In the hands of a capable driver it is a wonderful machine, but one must remember that when the desired amount of lock is obtained the lever must be put back to central position to hold that lock. To change the lock the lever is moved accordingly and returned to centre. The driver must also remember that the further he pushes the lever from centre the faster will go the steerage engine. If the driver should do this, and forget to bring the lever to the central position, the engine continues on until full lock is obtained. It then hits the safety catch which throws the steerage lever in the opposite direction, thus obtaining full lock the other way.

This cycle will continue until the unfortunate driver is able to catch the fast oscillating lever and hold it in the neutral position. Only then will this whirring mass of machinery come to a halt. All this is most disconcerting, especially if it should happen on the highway, as I was destined to find out.

The throttle of the main engine is a large wheel-valve, situated within easy reach of the driver's left hand.

By the time I arrived at the yard, the driver was already there, with a full head of steam, ready and waiting. After a brief discussion with the foreman fitter, I signalled the driver to take her out of the yard on to the main road. He appeared to hesitate for a moment, then climbed into the driving seat with, I thought, a certain amount of trepidation. He then put the reverse lever into forward gear, opened up the throttle, and shot forward like a bullet from a gun. With a resounding " crash " he hit a steam roller standing some few yards ahead of him. Without closing the throttle, he pulled the reversing lever back, and shot backwards into a living van. Undaunted he pushed the reverse lever forward again, with the throttle still open ; then, for some reason unknown to himself or anyone else, he touched the steering lever, that miraculously took him on to the right lock and charged forward in a graceful curve until stopped, with an almighty " BOOM," by the oak gatepost.

At this juncture I deemed it expedient to stop the general slaughter and, walking over, I asked him (quite politely) if this was his usual procedure to gain access to the highway. His reply was most fluent, but absolutely unprintable. By knowing the language I was able to translate it to mean that if I thought I could do any better I had his full permission to do so !

77

Catching the eye of the foreman fitter, who by now had been joined by two apprentices and the boilersmith—to say nothing of the onlookers outside, I thought I detected the flicker of a smile, meaning " Now we are going to see something." Determined not to lose prestige, or suffer damage to my ego, I climbed to the driving seat and whispered a silent prayer for guidance. Anyone more unlike a roller driver than me I cannot imagine ; wearing a bowler hat, white shirt and collar, spotted bow-tie, blue suit, black shoes with grey spats, and a blue raincoat which I handed to the fitter's mate, together with my silver-mounted walking stick and kid gloves.

Taking my courage in both hands, I pulled the reversing lever back. Then, very very gently opened the throttle. To my utter amazement the engine turned quite slowly and back we rolled. Gaining confidence, I experimented with the steering, gently easing the lever back, the engine slowly turning the fork to the required lock.

At this point I felt quite capable of taking the roller on to the road outside the yard, despite the sardonic smile on the face of the onlookers. The Gods were with me. I reached the road and turned in the direction of Kingston station without mishap, then brought her to a halt for the purpose only of time to gain confidence.

By this time quite a crowd had gathered to see the fun. Slowly I opened the throttle again and rolled away at about 1½ miles an hour, followed by the foreman fitter and the mystified driver.

I began to get quite brave, and opened up to about four miles an hour. All went well, until it became necessary to avoid a stationary baker's van. I pulled the steering lever back to turn out to the right but, alas, too far. The steering engine whizzed round to full lock, hit the safety catch, knocking the lever from my hand, and started up the cycles already referred to. Frantically, I tried to catch the flying lever and in my frenzy, I forgot to close the throttle. At this inopportune moment the "Pop" type safety valve opened with a deafening roar. Amid a cloud of steam and still doing a good four miles an hour, but now in series of graceful curves across the road and back I continued.

Yells of delight came from the kids following in the road behind me. In some inexplicable way I managed to regain my self-control and remembered to close the main steam valve. Slowly the roller came to a halt. The " Pop " safety valve snapped shut and a deathly silence fell upon all.

Only when the steam had cleared did I see that I had pulled

up a few feet into the main Kingston to Ham road, to the great consternation of the traffic using the down side, and for that matter the upside, of the road too. Here and now do I thank the Lord for one understanding policeman on traffic control, for this very busy thoroughfare had to be crossed to gain access to the Kingston goods yard. Realising my difficulty, having seen these juggernauts before, he held up all traffic going in either direction to allow me to slowly very slowly cross the road.

Reaching the sanctuary of the station approach, I stopped and breathed a sigh of relief. Mission safely accomplished—well, except for knocking down a white board in the middle of the main road with some sort of notice on it, but what matter a notice board in a crisis !

I did eventually get the roller loaded on to a railway truck, but just how, I will never know.

So, if anyone should ask me now, " Do I know anything about steam rollers ? " the answer is definitely " NO," and if I had to drive one of the tandem type, I'd rather be back at sea again, it would be much safer.

The driver, that should have been, after the roller had been loaded, asked me " Have you ever driven one of these rollers before, Sir ? "

" No." I replied truthfully.

" Neither have I," said he, then walked off into the gloom, presumably to look for another job.

While on the subject of steam rollers, it calls to mind the story of an old fellow in our village, Bill Sparkes, by name, a general labourer who would undertake to do any job within his very limited capabilities.

He had been offered the job of " Flagman " by a firm of rolling contractors to " Flag " one of their rollers moving from one job to another some miles away. The unexpected adventure, with dire consequences to the roller, can only be told at its best in his own words. In broad Sussex dialect.

Bill, seated in his favourite corner by the fire in the pub one evening, eyed his half-empty beer mug dolefully, hoping that it would be filled free of charge by his forthcoming announcement.

" Wun't be seeing ya fur a week or two, a'ter tomorrow," he announced to the landlord.

" Oh ! where you goin' then ? "

"Got a job," answered Bill, "gwain 'long with a steam roller. Dunno when I'll be back." Bill drains his mug, and since there is no sign of it being refilled free says good night, and leaves for home. Four days later he is back again and seated in his usual corner.

"Thought you got a job, Bill," says the landlord.

"Ahh," replied Bill, "so I 'ad. Got the —— sack too."

"'owever was that," asked the landlord.

"Wull," said Bill, "We gets 'alfway there, an' pulls in fur the night 'longside the road, an' old George, the driver he says, I'm gwain 'ome fur the night, ('cos 'e lives not fur 'way, see). I'm gwain 'ome fur the night 'e says. Stoke 'er up 'fore you turns in, so's we got steam in the morning. Alright George, I says, I'll see to 'er. So off 'e goos."

"A'ter I'd 'ad my supper I went out and stoaked 'er up. Then I turns in. I wakes up in the night and there she was a-hissin' an' a-spittin' and a-splutterin'. I says to myself ' Sounds as if she's gwain to bile o'er ' so I gets out, an' I clambers up into the old tank place, an' I pulls one 'andle, an' I pulls another, an' I kep' on pullin', till presen'ly damned if she didn't start gwain. Wull, I didn't know 'ow to stop 'er, so I clambered out an' let the old —— goo. She run 'long the road, then went arse-over-'ead in the dick, an' there she bid. She didn't blow up though ; presen'ly she stopped blowing off steam so I turned in again. Took us two days to get 'er out, an' then gives me the —— sack, so I come back 'ome."

13

The first of our
steam wagons

SOON AFTER father's death, when Cyril had accustomed himself to the managerial duties, he became keenly interested in the capabilities of the steam wagon. Seeing an advertisement in a machinery magazine offering a steam wagon and trailer for sale in Lewisham, he decided to go and have a look at it. It transpired to be a 1914 Clayton and Shuttleworth two-speed 5-ton wagon and a Clayton trailer, both being fitted with steel tyres on wooden wheels. They had been most carefully maintained and were found to be in perfect condition. Cyril bought the set, engaging the old driver to bring the whole outfit back to our yard, and giving him the option of joining our staff if he so wished, an offer he gladly accepted.

She was put to work immediately, and for several months all went well, the wagon and Sam Barton, her driver doing a wonderful job. Then one day in December of 1918, Sam was travelling from Fisher Lane to Cranleigh station with a load of pit-props, doing his usual 5-6 miles an hour. As he came to the brow of a short steep hill, with a small bridge at the bottom, he saw in front of him a few yards ahead a horse-drawn Gipsy caravan right in the middle of the road.

There being no room to pass on either side of the caravan, Sam jabbed his foot hard down on the pedal of the flywheel brake, yanking the reversing lever back at the same time in a desperate effort to stop the wagon. Unfortunately the road was covered with wet mud, left by the wheels of farm carts going in and out of a field nearby. As the steel tyres of the wagon caught the mud she went into a sideway skid and careered on crabwise down the hill, catching the gipsy caravan a glancing blow which capsized it into the ditch. Tin pans, kettles, brooms and clothes pegs flew in all directions, to the accompaniment of shouting and cursing from the gipsy owner.

At this point Sam's fireman decided that it was time to abandon ship and jumped clear, leaving Sam to fend for himself as best he could. A few yards further on the wagon hit the parapet of the bridge broadside on, cutting the brickwork for six. She finally came to rest at an alarming angle with her front wheels overhanging the stream, discharging with a dreadful rumbling the greater part of her load of pit-props into the water below. Sam emerged from the wreckage all in one piece, rubbing his leg and volubly cursing gipsies and their caravans to all eternity.

When the news of the accident reached the office at home, the Burrell tractor was dispatched to the scene with timbers, jacks, and chains. After two days of hard toiling in bitterly cold weather, the Clayton wagon was lifted clear of the bridge and towed back to the yard.

At this point, I must explain, my mother and Cyril had prevailed upon me to leave the firm of rolling contractors, with whom I had been engaged while taking a break from sea-going to rejoin the family business and take up duties at home as engineer, cum driver, cum office-boy, cum everything else. My first job was to help repair the damage to the Clayton wagon incurred in the accident mentioned above. Incidentally, it almost proved to be my last.

Among the many repairs to the wagon, was that of the water tank. Through its contact with the parapet of the bridge, the bottom had been ripped open. A new plate had been cut to shape, drilled and fitted, and was now held in place with a few bolts ready for riveting.

Then came the question ; who was going inside the tank to put the rivets in and to " dolly " up the heads ? Now mother nature having endowed me with a sylph-like figure, six feet in height, and the rest of the gang in the yard with girths far greater than mine, it therefore fell to my lot to remove my jacket and crawl through the manhole of the tank. This I was able to do with comparative ease, if with some reluctance.

After an hour inside the tank the heat became unbearable, so I announced my intention of coming out for a " breather." Owing

Sam ploughs his way through the bridge. (*Drawing by the author*).

to the heat, and my cramped position, my body had swollen to such an extent as to make it impossible for me to wriggle back out. Though my legs protruded from the manhole, the rest of me flatly refused to come through.

At first everyone in the yard thought it a huge joke, and many crude remarks were made at my expense, until the full gravity of the situation became apparent. Cyril was called from the office, and he and Bob Hooker pulled at my legs, but all to no avail, my backside stubbornly refused to come through the manhole. At Cyril's request I undid my braces ; my overalls, trousers, and under-pants were then pulled off, leaving my bare legs and after end exposed to the world. Again they pulled at my legs, and still I remained stuck fast. By this time considerable amounts of skin had been removed from my hips by the sharp edges of the manhole.

Bob then came up with what he called a brilliant suggestion ; that of covering my, now very tender behind, with grease. Cyril pondered this for a moment, then enquired of me what I thought of the idea. " I don't care what the hell you do," said I, " So long as you get me out of this —— tank."

Quickly a tin was brought from the store, and my posterior was plastered with grease to the tune of ribald jesting from our black-smith, who could no longer restrain his mirth at seeing my bare legs and part of my bottom sticking out of the manhole.

When the greasing had been completed, Bob and Cyril again. pulled at my legs, while Bert, the blacksmith, prized down the rolls of flesh on my rump with a tyre lever, accompanied by plenty of shouting from me requesting him to go easy with the lever. At last, to my unbounded relief, I was pulled clear, and I assure you, that nothing on earth would persuade me to go back into the tank again. Little wonder that I now suffer with claustrophobia. To finish the riveting we had to enlist the help of a little old fellow who worked on a nearby farm.

Before the repairs to the wagon were completed, greater troubles were to come to me. The front and hind wheels of the wagon had been removed for the purpose of having them converted to " press-on " rubber tyres, and also the back axle for differential repairs. The back of the wagon was now temporarily supported by a large baulk of timber resting on two steel drums.

To replace the now finished water tank it became necessary to jack up the back of the wagon an inch or so to allow it to slide under the chassis. It was then pushed under and levered up into its position between the carrier slings.

At this point I crawled under the wagon to put the nuts on to the slings. As I was doing this I thought I detected a slight movement of the engine above me. After waiting a few moments, I came to the conclusion that it must have been my eyes playing tricks with me, and I continued to put on the nuts. Then to my horror, the wagon gave a terrifying lurch, the two bottle screw-jacks skidded sideways, and the wagon came crashing down to the ground, knocking away the timber and drums as it fell, trapping me beneath it.

My left leg was caught beneath the water tank, and the cross-member of the chassis bore down on my shoulders, bending me double " jack-knife " fashion. Mercifully the wagon in falling had fouled a large baulk of timber, thereby affording me about eighteen inches in which to survive.

The noise made by the crash brought everyone in the yard and Cyril from the office running to my assistance, all fully convinced that I had been killed. Cyril crawled under the mass of ironwork, as he got near to me he spoke, but I could not answer him, I could only move one of my hands to touch his. As I did so he cried out to all the others waiting near at hand, " Thank God he is still alive," then rushed to organise my rescue.

My sister, who worked in the office, upon hearing the sound of the crash, then Cyril's cry of joy at finding me still alive, ran back to the office and telephoned for a doctor, who now stood close by waiting for me to be brought out.

The position in which I was trapped with my head forced hard down upon one knee, made it impossible for me to see what was going on. I could only hear my rescuers working feverishly with jacks and timbers to raise the wagon sufficiently for my release. I don't remember feeling any pain. My only thought was that in their desperate endeavours to free me the wagon might slip from the greasy baulk of timber that stood between me and certain death.

When at last I was dragged clear, after what seemed an eternity to me, and the doctor's first full examination of me was over, of which I remember very little, I was gently slid on to a wide plank and taken to my home with a broken leg and severe damage to the lower part of the vertebrae through being bent double. The latter gave me a stoop that I carry to this day.

Many of our employees called to see me during my convalescence, among them was our fitter, Bob Hooker. According to Bob's reckoning it was one of two things to which I owed my life; it was either the devil looking after his own, or I had quite a bit of the cat about me, or I would surely have been kiilled. There may have been a heck of a lot of truth in his reckoning, I don't know. If it were the former, well, that's fair enough, but if the latter, I'm wondering how many of the nine lives I've got left . . . .

14

Hay for the military

BY 1919 we had acquired our second steam wagon, a new Clayton and Shuttleworth, two-speed, 5 ton, chain steerage model, mounted on rubber tyres, a similar type to our first wagon, except that she was fitted with a geared-down boiler feed pump, a slightly higher top gear ratio, and a greater capacity water tank. Upon her delivery to our yard I was appointed as her driver.

About this time we had entered into a contract with a firm of hay and straw merchants, for the cartage of these commodities into the Aldershot Barracks from various farms in Surrey and Sussex.

After a fortnight or so on this work with the Clayton No. 2, Tiny Hardman, my fireman, and I were really getting the hang of things regarding the loading and transportation of trussed hay.

One day, as we pulled into a farm near Worplesdon, near Guildford, Tiny jumped down from the tender of the wagon to guide me into the stack yard, to where a thirty ton pile of neatly cut trusses of hay stood stacked.

" By 'ell guv'ner," remarked Tiny, as he stood looking at the hay, " This is the best we've ever 'ad, and all square cut too. We shouldn't 'ave any trouble with this lot."

" Umm ! " I retorted, " I wouldn't be so sure of that." I knew only too well the idiosyncrases of the Fodder Officers and the inexplicable verdicts given by them regarding your load of hay or straw. As for a load of hay; it could be as unpredictable as a bee in a jam-

87

pot, you never knew what it would do, whether it would remain peacefully on the wagon or scatter itself along the road.

Machine bailers of course were known, and used, in 1919, but mostly trusses were cut from a rick of hay with a " swaith knife," weighed to 56 lbs., pressed in a lever press and tied by hand with hay cord. A " Hay Tier," as he was known, could, by the degree of his skill, make or mar the appearance of the hay, and of course, your load.

Ten o'clock in the morning was the deadline for inspection parade at the barracks, and with our first load from this farm we arrived in good time. Passing over the weighbridge with the wagon and trailer, we were given our weight ticket and sent on to rendezvous with the inspection officers. We found ourselves fifth in the queue of about thirty wagons of various makes.

After we had waited for half an hour or so, a group of officers arrived headed by a major, with a sergeant in the rear. The sergeant was armed with what looked like an overgrown corkscrew, and at the command of the major he twisted it into a truss on our load specified by him. As it was withdrawn, a wisp of hay came out with it from the centre of the truss. This he disentangled from the corkscrew and handed to the major, who smelt it, twisted it, smelt it again, then started to chew a piece of it. He handed the wisp of hay to the others and in each in turn followed the same procedure. With a curt nod of the head by all of them, it was deemed fit for army equine consumption. Briskly the sergeant stepped up to us and told us where it was to be unloaded. This ritual was methodically carried out with every load that was taken into the barracks.

Experience had taught us, that if we were among the first fifteen wagons in the queue, we stood a 99% chance of our load being passed.

For a few loads from the farm at Worplesdon all went well. Then, one morning, as we were travelling toward the barracks, we were amazed to see a car pull alongside and slow down to our speed, the driver frantically sounding his Klaxon Horn and pointing upwards.

" What the 'ell's up with him ? " shouted Tiny in my ear.

" Dunno," I replied, shrugging my shoulders. Stopping the wagon, I jumped to the ground to ascertain the cause of the car driver's agitation. As I walked round and looked in the direction indicated, I saw a haze of smoke going up from the top of the load on the wagon. Despite the precaution of sheets to protect the hay against such an event, and the use of a very efficient spark arrester, we were on fire.

" Blimey," I yelled to Tiny, " We're alight."

Within seconds he was by my side and the pair of us shinned up the holding down ropes like a couple of monkeys, treading madly on the smouldering cloth to extinguish the fire.

Fortunately for us the hay was not really damaged, but merely charred in that one spot. This portion we scratched away, and felt quite sure it would pass the inspection parade undetected.

The delay, however, caused us to be well to the back end of the queue, and the verdict of the fodder officers was, as we feared, " NOT PASSED."

" Now what the devil do we do ? " asked Tiny in alarm.

" Well. I guess there is nothing for it but to contact the agent," I answered somewhat dejectedly. Pulling out of the barracks gate to the main road, I stopped at the nearest Post Office to use the telephone. I explained to him the predicament we were in. He laughed heartily, and told us to return to the farm and take the same load in again the next morning. This we did, arriving at the barracks very early to find ourselves first in the queue, and to our great relief our load was accepted.

A few days after this, we really had our Hey (Hay ?) day. We were making good time on this particular morning and had reached the centre of Aldershot Town. On rounding a bend in the road in front of the Hippodrome I became aware of people on the footway gaping at our load open-mouthed and all traffic coming to a halt. Sensing what was wrong I eased back the regulator pulled slowly to the curb and stopped. Jumping down from my driving position I walked round to the side of the wagon to see how bad the situation really was.

The sight that greeted me was a far from pleasant one, for our trailer load had taken on a terrifying list toward the centre of the road. This in itself was bad enough, but festooned along the side of the load was the tattered remains of someone's shop blind, with the word " Lingerie " emblazoned thereon in large black letters, while from a long streamer of canvas trailed the blind roller.

Tiny had by now got down from the tender of the wagon and was standing by my side. " Blimey guv'ner," he murmured, scratching the back of his neck thoughtfully, " This ain't our day, is it ? "

Powerless to do anything to prevent the load falling we stood

Consternation—and hay—abound in Aldershot. (*Drawing by Miss A. Child*).

and watched, as in slow motion the list grew steadily worse, then "WHOOSH" and two thirds of the hay cascaded into the busy street. In gay abandon trusses bounced and bumped in all directions, some bursting their bonds en route and sending up a terrific shower of hay seeds as the cords gave way.

Within seconds we were surrounded by policemen, all complete with note books at the ready and each asking the same darn silly questions. Only one had the brain wave to contact the Borough Council for help to clear the highway, and enable the traffic to get moving again.

While dealing with the police, I caught sight of a rotund little man dressed in striped trousers and a black morning coat, hurrying toward us, mopping his bald head with a large handerchief, and shouting, "I'll have the law on you for this," To which Tiny's rejoinder was, "You're too —— late guv'ner. We've already got 'em on us."

Since he proved to be the owner of the shop blind, he was given our address by the police and informed that the matter would be dealt with in due course.

What hay could be retrieved was reloaded onto the trailer, roped down and sheeted, but it was a sorry looking load that pulled into the barracks the next morning. Needless to say, it was rejected out of hand. I telephoned the agent and explained what had happened "Ah well," said he, unperturbed at the news, "Take it on to the Remount Depot at Arborfield."

After driving like mad to get there before the depot closed for the day, we reached the main gate and pulled into the courtyard of the hay store. The officer in charge came out of his office, took one look at our load, cursed us profusely for wasting his time, and told us to get out of it, or words to that effect.

Tiny and I by this time were becoming a little despondent, and a review of our coal situation did nothing to cheer us up.

Pulling out of the Remount Depot we drew into the forecourt of a nearby pub. Here I left Tiny in charge of the wagon while I went to arrange for a supply of coal to be brought out to us in the morning from Reading, and also to enquire of the agent regarding our further instructions. These were to take the hay on to Messrs. So and So's Store at Kingston-on-Thames.

Our coal being delivered to us by 7.30 the next morning we were soon on our way to Kingston. We arrived there late in the afternoon, only to be told that their store was full, and that they could not accept delivery. This, as far as I was concerned, was the end. Using language that is reserved solely for the use of nautical gentlemen and timber hauliers, I made my way to the telephone to contact the agent once again. The female voice at the other end of the line informed me that he had left the office, and could she help me? I explained what had happened. "Oh dear," came the reply. "In that case you'd better take it on to the A.B.C. Stables at Epsom." Here, I regret to say, my patience finally deserted me. "Will I —— hell," I exploded, then biting my tongue to remind myself that I must not use bad language over the telephone, I continued, "I'm taking it to the nearest railway goods yard, loading it onto a goods wagon and consigning it to Hades."

"Please don't do that," piped the anxious voice in all seriousness, "We haven't got a customer there. Send it to our depot in Bermondsey." Bermondsey or Hades, it was all one to me, I was fed to the teeth with it. So came the end of day number three with that load, and so to bed, curled up in the hay under the cloth. Early the next morning it was loaded into a goods wagon, and by heaven, we were pleased to see the end of it.

When the last load had been taken from the farm at Worplesdon, the next job was twenty-five tons of straw to be taken to the barracks from a farm at Ebernoe, near Petworth.

On the evening after our first load of straw had been delivered my brother Cyril came out in the Overland car to where Tiny and I were in lodgings, bringing with him a supply of cylinder and bearing oil for the wagon, our wages for the week, and three pounds for my use to purchase coal and other incidentals that might be required during our work away from home.

"Now," said Cyril, after he had settled the money problems. "When you have delivered your load of straw tomorrow, I want you to go straight through to Guildford Gas works, load up as much coke breeze as you can get on the wagon and trailer, and take it to Manford's Brick Yard, Cranleigh. It's desperately urgent, so get through with it even if it is after midnight."

"O.K.," said I lightheartedly, "We'll be there."

If the distance from farm to barracks was such as to make it impossible to attend the 10 o'clock parade, arrangements could be made with the Quarter Master Sergeant to be included in the limited number of wagons that were allowed in the afternoon inspection.

92

Our Ebernoe journey enabled us to qualify for this, so on the morning following Cyril's overnight instructions, Tiny and I were early at the farm to load the straw.

I lit the fire in the engine, in order to raise steam while we were loading. When the load on the wagon had been completed, a start was made to load the trailer. It was now nine o'clock, and we stopped for lunch. I climbed down from the half-loaded trailer to join Tiny, who was sitting on a truss of straw, to eat our food together. At this moment the farmer came over to us to enquire if we would like a glass of mead with our food. I thanked him politely and replied that we would.

" I'll send the girl over with it," said he, turning on his heel and walking back to the house. A few minutes later the maid came out to us carrying a pint jug and two glasses.

" Struth," remarked Tiny, eyeing the jug critically, and looking up at the girl he continued, " 'e didn't mean us to have too much, did 'e ? "

" Boss has gone to market," she said shyly to Tiny, " So when you've finished that I'll get you some more." I handed her the empty jug, and true to her word she returned a few minutes later with it refilled.

" It's the first time I've tasted mead," remarked Tiny to me, licking his lips, " Good ain't it," I agreed with him whole-heartedly. " It's the first time I've tasted it too, but come on, let's finish loading or we'll be late."

I then made up the fire in the engine, and after using the injector to put more water into the boiler, I closed the damper, and climbed a little unsteadily back on to the half-loaded trailer.

Tiny, picking up his prong, jabbed it viciously into a truss of straw, and after a few false starts managed to get it up to where I was standing. With the next truss however he seemed to experience some difficulty in spearing it at all. When at last he did get the prong into it, and with superhuman effort got the handle on to his shoulder, he made one lurch toward the trailer, then suddenly went into reverse, ran backwards for a few steps and fell flat on his back, out for the count.

Beginning now to feel the effect of the mead myself, I crawled to the side of the load to see what had happened to Tiny, but unfortunately I must have got too near to the edge and went slithering headlong into the straw on the ground below.

At about three that afternoon I awoke with the feeling that I was chained to the ground, and with a buzzing in my head that sounded like a million bees cavorting in at one ear and out of the other. I remembered vaguely that I was in charge of a steam wagon. In desperation I half crawled, half staggered toward her and somehow managed to climb into the tender, only to find that there was no steam, no water showing in the gauge glass, and the fire gone out completely. Finding my tea bottle I took a long drink from it, then fell backwards out of the tender to the ground and sank once more into oblivion.

Some hours later I became aware of being shaken violently, and of water from a cold wet sponge being splashed on my face. When at last I opened my eyes I found myself looking up into the extremely angry face of my brother Cyril, who, fearing an accident had befallen us, had travelled our route in the reverse direction in an effort to locate us. I couldn't even try to tell you what he called Tiny and me, but I assure you it was far from complimentary.

Tiny and I, still too drunk to walk, were carried to Cyril's car and bundled unceremoniously into it, to be driven to our respective homes, poor Tiny to be given notice to quit, and I a severe reprimanding.

Two days later, when I had regained my normal state of health, I walked briskly into the office. " Is it true that you have sacked Tiny ? " I demanded of Cyril.

" Yes," he replied sternly, not taking his eyes from the letter he was reading.

" Right," I spat out, turning to walk out of the office door, " He was the best mate I ever worked with, so count me as sacked too ! "

Cyril spun round in his chair, jumped to his feet, calling me several different sorts of a young fool and dragged me back into the office again, and the devil's own argument ensued between us. Finally my mother and sister were called in to mediate between us. The pros and cons were weighed (and probably found wanting on my side) with the result that Tiny was reinstated, and I withdrew my resignation, and our little world continued to revolve peacefully once more.

Even today, if I should see or pass a load of straw, I seem to hear bees buzzing and see a jug of mead. Queer ! Ain't it ?

15

" Bumping " in the '20's

THE USUAL Sunday morning's boiler wash-out was going on in the yard, and hearing a strange voice I looked up from my job of repacking the feed pump of No. 1 Clayton Wagon, and saw a sparsely built, military looking man, a complete stranger.

He was directed over to me by one of our men, and as he approached me, he enquired whether it were possible on a Sunday morning, to see the manager ? I informed him that my brother, the manager, was not available, but that I was a member of the firm, and could I help him ?

His speech declared him to be one of the aristocracy without a doubt, but his mode of dress struck me, to say the least, a little odd. He wore a pair of heavy boots, covered in mud, a suit of Plus Fours frayed at the elbows and cuffs, and he wore a Deer Stalker cap covered in fish hooks and flies, as well as using a long thumbedstick.

Not being used to this form of attire, I had the feeling that I was dealing with a gentleman who was perhaps a little unbalanced and when he stated his request, i.e., transport for sixty boxes of clothing, I felt that I was correct in my assumption.

Upon enquiring as to whom I was addressing, he informed me that he was the Marquis of "X." This, of course, was the end. I politely said that I was delighted to meet him, and (not to be outdone) told him I was the Shah of Persia. He smiled, but said nothing, then he handed me a piece of paper with an address, where, if we were interested, we might view the goods.

95

My brother and I, later, drove out to the address given, and on ringing the bell, the door was opened by a butler. We informed him that we were expected, and when he bade us enter, saying that he would inform his Lordship, the bottom fell right out of my stomach. " Great Scott," I thought, " he really is a Marquis ! "

His lordship walked straight up to me, his hand outstretched, a broad grin on his face, saying, " Ah, my dear friend the Shah of Persia, do come in."

The sixty boxes of clothes transpired to be the complete household to be removed from Knightons to Strathfield Saye, the family seat.

The first journey was done with the Clayton No. 2, and consisted of three-and-a-half miles of wire netting. We loaded up on a Monday evening in August 1920, and started for Strathfield Saye the following morning. All went well, until we were climbing Castle Hill, Farnham, where the camber of the road encouraged about a mile of the wire netting, in rolls, to cascade down the hill. This had to be retrieved and reloaded.

Roping down again, more securely, we went on our way, having lost several hours. Night was falling before we reached Odiham. A little uncertain of our way, I asked a passer-by, who gave us our direction. Either he was wrong, or I too was tired to count the turnings correctly, for we found ourselves in a narrow lane, with a gate barring our further way. We had turned down a farm entrance and found ourselves in the farmyard with no room to turn round.

After a lot of persuasion, we got the farmer to harness up two horses, and tow our trailer backwards into a field entrance, then reversing the wagon, we towed the trailer, on the head coupling, to the main road. All this in the dark, before the moon rose.

After one or two other mishaps, we finally arrived at a crossroads on what appeared to be a vast common. There was no sign post to indicate our way, so I decided to send my fireman down one road, our mate down another, and I took the third, in search of a house, or someone to tell us where we were.

After going about fifty yards down my road, I saw, in the moonlight, the road stretching away in the distance, and with no sign of life anywhere, decided to return to the wagon.

It was, by now, about one o'clock in the morning, so we decided to wait till daybreak and the first passer-by.

Forethought on our mate's part saved the supper situation.

He had brought along with him a half-pound of sausages, which we cooked in the fire shovel over the fire in the box and shared out.

The first light of dawn revealed our way, the long straight road turned out to be a tall white monument at the entrance gate to our journey's end.

So much time having been lost en route, our coal bunker was empty, so we decided to use a bag from our return supply in the trailer Alas ! although there were five hundredweights of the stuff, it was buried beneath the wire netting. There was nothing for it but to pick up the wood from the roadside. Poor stuff for steaming, but it enabled us to complete the last three-quarters of a mile to our destination.

We returned the following day to Knightons, for load number two.

Load number two consisted, as indeed did three, four and five, entirely of furniture, which had in the meantime been listed and numbered, whilst on the other side of the inventory, a corresponding number told our packers to which particular room the article was to be delivered. For this and further loads, a lift box was placed on the wagon, and a Pantechnicon in place of the trailer. Our party now consisted of myself as driver, my fireman, two packers, and one of the Marquis' old retainers as guard.

Nothing of note happened on this journey. We arrived at our destination, and unloaded in one day, returning to Knightons the following afternoon.

Load number three proved a little more exciting. My brother had decided to give a hand with the packing, incidentally making a first class job of it, until a large case of butterflies was brought out from the study. These, apparently, had great sentimental value, and strict instructions were given for the utmost care to be taken for their safe transit. They were laid on the floor, whilst my brother made a suitable " bed " for them, on top of the stacked furniture. Stepping backwards to pick up the case, he put his foot straight through the glass. To the accompaniment of falling pieces, came the voice of his lordship, who had chosen this unfortunate moment to call on us to see what progress was being made. " Is everything all right ? " he enquired. My brother, his foot still among the butterflies, replied (or perhaps I should have said " lied,") " Perfectly, your lordship, perfectly." Mercifully, his lordship's quick departure enabled the transference of the butterfly case from the van to my brother's car, and off to our yard, where with the help of our carpenter and an entomologist friend, the damaged case was repaired and the mutilated flies placed once more above their respective names. By-the-way, if you should ever be fortunate enough to see these butterflies, please refrain from saying too much about them should you notice one or two with " odd " wings.

As I have already said, load number three was a little more exciting. Loading completed, we started away, covering only six miles when, to my horror, the h.p. slide valve rod broke. 1 tried the old trick of pushing the regulator onto the double high side, but with the double high valve lever still in the compound position. This enabled me to pull off the road, but the heavy blast up the chimney made it impossible to travel far. Our Burrell 6 h.p. traction was called to haul us back to the yard for repair. Since the repair was not completed before midday on the Friday, it was decided to leave the load in the yard over the weekend.

Soon after lunch on the Saturday following the repair, a sergeant of police, called upon us to enquire, in typical police sergeant style, as to the whereabouts of a certain box, said to be marked number . . . and reported to them, the police, as undelivered to its rightful owner.

We were at a loss to understand what all this was about. However the inventory was produced, and it was discovered that the said box was still on the wagon. Although numbered, no indication was given as to its contents, but a telephone call soon settled this problem. Seemingly, the box contained a great part of the family plate, of no mean value, so a guard had to be put on duty over the weekend.

Such were the tribulations of " Furniture Bumping."

Load number three finished without further incident, as did numbers four and five.

Incidently, whenever his lordship had occasion to speak to me, which was frequently, he always referred to me as " My dear friend the Shah."

16

The wagon rolls westward

A LETTER from the Aldershot command bore no great significance; they were frequent enough at our office, as over the years many haulage jobs had been carried out for it. So when my brother Cyril handed me a letter from the command received by the morning post, I felt no cause for alarm. As I took it from him he watched my face, waited until I had read it, then enquired ; " What do you make of that lot ? " I handed the missive back to him with a non-committal " UMM," adding, " I wonder what all that's about."

The letter was stamped outside and inside " Priority Urgent." The wording was simple, so was the request. It merely asked for the supply of suitable transport for the conveyance of some 50 cases of unspecified goods. It gave no indication as to destination other than a few miles out of Bristol, and the weight we were to carry was just as vague—about 6 to 10 tons. More stress seemed to be laid on the fact that the vehicle must be rubber tyred and well sprung.

The driver, the letter stated, must report to the officer commanding heavy artillery, Aldershot, where orders would be given in detail.

As Cyril took the letter from my hand a broad grin spread over his face. " This looks as though it might be a pleasant Sunday afternoon mystery tour. I think you'd better do it with No. 2 Clayton wagon and trailer," he remarked.

During the past few days No. 2 Clayton had undergone certain repairs and modifications, among them an alteration to the

99

flywheel brake to make it more efficient. This brake was operated by the driver by means of a foot pedal. New hardwood blocks had also been fitted to the band brake that worked on a drum keyed to the back axle. This brake when required was applied by the fireman by a handwheel in the wagon cab. Another addition was a handwheel by the driver's position to apply the trailer's brake. With all these jobs done I felt she could be driven to Timbuktu, let alone to Bristol.

The contract tender was accepted by the Aldershot command and a date for the journey fixed. On the evening previous to starting, my fireman Tiny Hardman and I bunkered the Clayton with coal and water. Two extra bags of coal were placed on the rack on top of the cab together with 1 gallon of cylinder oil, 1½ gallons of bearing oil, a tin of grease, the tube brush and the usual clinkering tools. The trailer was coupled up and all was made ready for an early start the next morning.

We left the yard at Alfold soon after 5 a.m. on a beautiful morning in June of 1920 to make the journey to Aldershot, where we arrived without incident just after 9 a.m.

I reported to the address as requested, and after waiting two or three hours received orders to go to Bramley, near Basingstoke, there to report to the officer in charge of munitions.

Bramley was reached in the late afternnon. I was then told that we were to go to shed No. — where the wagon and trailer would be loaded with straw, that Sergeant X would go with me and that we were to return to Bay No. — after loading.

This accomplished we returned to the bay where I was told to leave the wagon for the night. My fireman and I were then led off to the Sergeant's Mess, fed, given blankets and allocated a place to sleep.

By this time it was getting late, and bed, however Army style, was very acceptable, but tired as I was my mind would not rest. Unanswerable questions kept going round in my brain. Why only a 12 inch layer of straw in the wagon and trailer ? Why couldn't the sergeant tell me what our load was to be ? Where was it to go ?

Five a.m. came all too soon. Tiny and I were brought back to life by a fearful blast on a bugle (or should I say blasted ?), and given a huge breakfast, after which we lit the fire to get steam in the wagon.

To my great astonishment I found that the wagon and trailer

had been loaded during the night and sheeted down with a kind of asbestos cloth.

Soon after we had lit the fire in the wagon, a sergeant and a corporal arrived carrying a small board, and a red flag fixed to a long stick. The sergeant handed me the flag with such solemnity that it might well have been the Regimental Colours, saying it must be fixed to the wagon cab in a prominent positon. He then gave me the board bearing the letters O.H.M.S., which had to be fixed over our number plate on the chimney base, covering our own registration. Seemingly O.H.M.S. held greater powers than our own index numbers.

I was then informed by the sergeant that both he and the corporal were to accompany us on the whole journey as " guards." When I asked him our destination, he replied ; " Your guess is as good as mine, mate." Both then walked to the back of the trailer, climbed aboard, sat down on the asbestos cloth and stared into space in stony silence.

" 'appy couple of blighters, ain't they," mused Tiny as we waited for instructions to move off. " I reckon they've just 'ad ten days C.B. for laughing."

Orders were eventually given for us to proceed to Kingsclere, where we were met by a dispatch rider on a motor cycle who gave us our directions to point " A." Here we were met by another who guided us to Burbage, where we were told to pull into a farm yard for the night. We were coaled-up and given food from a Peerless chain-driven 3 ton army lorry which was waiting for us there.

Naturally, when the meal was finished, I asked what accommodation had been provided for Tiny and me. I was quickly told in no uncertain way that on no account were we to leave the wagon throughout the whole journey. It was useless to argue, so the night was spent in fitful half-sleep in the coal bunker.

At five-thirty the next morning we pulled out of the farm. Following the directions given us we trundled our way to Market Lavington. Here again we were met by a dispatch rider who directed us down a road which he said would take us to point " B," a mile or so north of Westbury. (Points A, B, and so on, were where we were to be met by dispatch riders.)

Now there are A roads and B roads, but this one was lower than C class. The military authorities may be perfect in their organisation and secrecy, but for planning a route for an overloaded steam wagon I give them no marks at all. Gradients, up or down, were given no consideration whatsoever.

On we travelled toward point " B," overloaded as we were, having to change gear at every incline. Then we found a REAL gradient. I have no official record, but my memory makes it about 1 in 6. We were in fast wheel at the time and had no idea of what lay ahead of us round a sharp bend, but, believe me, we soon found out. The road, very narrow, just fell away, and down the hill we went like the clappers of hell.

Don't ask me what speed we reached; I have no idea. All I remember is the hill still going down and down and the wagon faster and faster. I stood on the flywheel brake pedal, steering with one hand and holding the reverse lever full back with the other. Tiny, meanwhile, was frantically winding on the wagon and trailer brakes, using a spanner for extra leverage on the former.

Blue smoke rolled up from everywhere, so much so from the flywheel brake that I had some difficulty in seeing the road. At last we reached the bottom and came sweating to a halt, only to be greeted with frantic yells from our sergeant who, with the corporal, were preparing for a hasty abandon ship. Smoke and flames rolled out from under the wagon. The back brake was on fire.

Tiny and I jumped simultaneously from the wagon, one armed with the fire shovel the other with the clinker shovel, to sling earth, dug from the side of the road, onto the burning brake. With the fire extinguished and our " guards " once more seated in their position on the trailer we moved on to rendezvous with the dispatch rider at Westbury. We finished the second day at a point four miles west of Westbury, parking for the night on a small green in the open country. Here coal and food had been left for us and again the night was spent in the coal bunker. The next morning saw us en route for Norton St. Philip.

As I have said, no thought had been given to hills or to our being able to pick up water. Since we had not been able to fill up over-night the tank was only half-full on our leaving in the morning. We travelled mile after mile with no sign of a stream or a pond. At last the injector spluttered and stopped working. The tank was empty.

A passing farm hand told us of a stream half a mile ahead. With a heavy load and only three quarters showing in the boiler gauge glass, my heart sank. Ever hopeful I opened the regulator to make a run for the stream, but the previous day's " hill do " had told its tale on the fusible plug. With that hissing sound in the firebox (hated so much by all steam drivers), we came to a halt some 200 yards from our watery goal.

This meant " firebox drill "—ashpan off, firebars out, unscrew fusible plug, a three mile walk to the nearest blacksmith to re-fill the plug with lead, the walk back, replace the refilled plug, firebars and ashpan, then fill the boiler, with only one bucket, from the stream.

All this resulted in several hours being lost. By the time steam was raised again it was late afternoon. We had only covered about 10 to 12 miles that day and finished a mile or so out of Norton St. Philip, thereby missing our rendezvous with the coal and food lorry. Once again the night was spent in the coal bunker but this time supperless. The sergeant and corporal, by the way, spent their nights on the boxes in the trailer, under the asbestos cloth.

Soon after dawn the next morning we were awakened by a dispatch rider saying he had been searching for us since 9 o'clock the evening before, and not having been given our route of the previous day by his predecessor, he had covered an area for miles around. A few minutes after his arrival the coal and food lorry turned up, and the supper missed the previous night was then rehashed as breakfast.

After oiling up the wagon we were on our way again making for Pensford, somewhere south-west of Bath. At this stage it occurred to me that we were carefully avoiding all towns and large villages by means of by-roads and lanes. But I still had no idea why.

The fourth day's run finished without mishap, except for the saddle brasses on the flywheel side continually heating up, due no doubt to the heavy braking during the hill epsiode. Rendezvous with the coal and food lorry was kept this time followed by the inevitable coalbunker sleep, and in the morning we continued our way to Downend. We were met there by another dispatch rider who this time stayed with us through Filton and down into Avonmouth Docks, waving all traffic into the side of the road, to afford us a clear passage through the town and over crossroads.

As we pulled into Avonmouth Docks, I was amazed to find a wharf completely cordoned off, in which no one except ourselves was allowed. This I proudly imagined was due to the magic O.H.M.S. on our chimney base. The only thing missing, according to Tiny, was a 21-gun salute.

An officer, no less than a major, guided us to the edge of the quay alongside an empty barge. Here, for some reason unknown to me, I was requested to draw the fire from the wagon, a tank half filled with water being provided to receive it.

With the fire drawn and completely extinguished, Tiny and I were led away to another part of the docks to be fed and given a bed for the night. What heaven after five days ! A real bed : a trifle hard perhaps, but infinitely better than the coal bunker.

The next morning we found the wagon and trailer empty. The sergeant and corporal, as well as the barge had gone. We were alone. Even the barricades had disappeared. The dock had resumed its everyday bustle. No one even threw a glance our way. I felt slightly wounded after our regal entry of the day before.

Before steam had been raised we were visited by an Army captain, who informed us that the mission was complete and that we were at liberty to leave. The red flag was hauled down, though permission was granted to retain the magic O.H.M.S. on our bows, as it would give us priority of the road through towns. But we were told that it must be returned to Aldershot immediately we had reached our destination.

By this time I was getting short of money and the ingenuity displayed by Tiny to obtain food, cigarettes and the odd glass of beer during the journey to Alfold is another story to be told.

Some two years later I had the good fortune to meet again the officer-in-charge of munitions, Bramley depot. " By the way," I enquired. " What the devil WAS in those cases we took to Avonmouth Docks ? "

" My dear boy," he replied grinning. " They were old and rusty shells, far too dangerous to be unloaded. The only thing we could do was to put them in that barge, tow it out to sea and sink the lot, barge and all. Wonderful job you did, my boy. Wonderful job."

A cold shiver ran down my spine. " Ah well," I said to myself, " ignorance sure is bliss." Thinking back, I have a feeling that our sergeant had no idea of the liveliness of our cargo either, or he would not have slept so peacefully on top of those cases . . .

Above: The firm's first Clayton & Shuttleworth, 1914, 5-ton steel-tyred steam wagon (later rubber tyred) (No. 1), hauling cord-wood to the mill. The rear tyre has been torn off by a tree root. (See p. 81). **Below:** This 1916 5-ton Foden wagon, taking hay into Aldershot Barracks, is typical of the many engaged on this work. (See pp. 87-91).

Above: The No. 2 Clayton & Shuttleworth 5-ton rubber-tyred steam wagon in the yard. On the left is " Tiny " Hardman. (See p. 87). **Below:** The old Burrell working at Newlands Corner. Note the water barrels, used after the tank had been damaged by the run-away (see p. 141).

17

The old rustic bridge

" NOVEMBER ain't my idear of the time o' year to shift saw' tackle," mused Bert Ewings, the driver of our 6 h.p. Burrell traction engine, half to himself, and half addressing me. " Mud up to your blasted eyeballs, saw-dust and wet clay everywhere. Look at my poor old ingin', just plastered with the flamin' stuff." He kicked out his feet alternately to rid them of the clinging mud, muttering curses with each kick as he clambered to the footplate of his engine.

" Never mind Bert," I laughed, " Mud is good for the complexion. Especially clay. You'll finish up with skin like a baby's after this." His only reply was another staggering outburst of cursing.

How I agreed with him. The weather was really appalling, raw, cold and damp. Everything one touched was wet through, even the tools one used had to be freed of mud before one could handle them. If a spanner, or other implement was accidentally dropped, the user would have to probe into the mud with a stick to find it again.

The work we were doing was the dismantling of one of our three bench sawmills, which had been in operation at this particular site for over two years. Now that the contract for sawmilling had come to an end, the mill had to be dismantled and taken back to our yard for overhaul before going on to the next estate contract.

For the transportation we had the Burrell 6 h.p. traction engine with two trucks, the Burrell tractor with one trailer, and the No. 2 Clayton wagon, which I was driving.

The Burrell traction was being used to load the sections of the dismantled sawmill and at this moment was about to winch the heavy centre piece of the rack-bench into one of the trucks. Three large baulks of timber had been placed from the ground to the floor of the truck, for this massive piece of equipment to slide up on. As it reached the floor the ends of the timber skids rose high into the air. I stepped forward with a heavy hammer to drive out a fouling wedge. As the rack centre slid into the truck the skids fell back to the ground with a tremendous " SPLOSH," sending out a colossal shower of mud which covered me from head to foot. I staggered back blindly and in so doing tripped over a chain, half hidden in the mud, falling full length into the slimy morass of clay.

It was now Bert's turn to laugh. " As you jus' said guv'ner, a mud bath's good for you, and I reckon as 'ow you enjoyed that'n." I swore lustily, cursing the mud and weather with every step I took on my way back to the Clayton wagon to clean myself down.

For two and a half days we had wallowed in mud and slime to load the mill machinery, until at last all was finished and we were ready to leave. The Burrell tractor, with the aid of a full set of paddles and her own winch, had extracted herself and her load from the mud bath on to the main road. Since she could be of no further help to us, she left for home some two or three hours before we were ready, two push-sawbenches and the corrugated iron sheets of the mill shed in her trailer, with a six-berth living van trailing behind.

The Burrell " tractor," classified as a " Motor " tractor legally was only allowed to tow any one vehicle mounted on two or four wheels behind it at a maximum speed of five miles per hour. There were times, however, when we would be prepared to argue that the speed had been reduced to four miles per hour and that the Burrell " tractor " was now a " light locomotive " and entitled to haul more than one trailer. Whether this argument would have held in a court of law, we were mercifully never called upon to prove, but it was worth the risk.

To return to the mud again. The Clayton wagon, now loaded with circular saws, crosscut saws, axes, belts, the mill countershaft gear and odds and ends of mill equipment, stood on a slab timber roadway, a five berth living van coupled behind, with a full head of steam ready to leave. Full of hope, and anxious to get away from this hellish sea of mud, I clambered to the driving position and gently opened the regulator to pull away. For a few yards the gods were kind to me. Then the near-side rear wheel began to slip on the greasy timber road, and in seconds skidded off the edge of the track to sink slowly and gracefully up to its axle in mud.

Bert, seeing my plight, came to my rescue by taking the Burrell traction out close to the main road. By the aid of his fifty yards of wire rope, hauled laboriously by seven of the mill men through mud, at times almost up to their knees, he was able to winch the Clayton wagon and the living van out on to firm ground. I breathed a sigh of relief.

Without further mishap, Bert was able to winch out his own two loaded trucks and the 10 h.p. Clayton portable mill engine to the main road, and couple up his train. The mill gang of twelve meanwhile gave a hand to clear the mud from our wheels and the roadway, so that by 1 p.m. we were on our way from the Aliceholt Forest to Alfold, and our yard.

When all was ready to move, I gave Bert instructions to go ahead of me while I followed close behind to be on hand in case of trouble of any kind. In procession we travelled on at four miles an hour through to Farnham. Soon after leaving the town we ran into patches of mist and after leaving the main London to Portsmouth road, darkness fell, adding a further hazard to the ever thickening fog. As we stopped to light our lamps, the fog really closed down upon us, making it impossible to see more than a few yards.

Whilst I was trying to get my tail lamp burning properly, Bert walked back to where I was standing. " We ain't goin' to make the yard tonight in this lot guv'ner," he said dejectedly, pulling his over-coat more closely about him in an effort to keep out the fog. " I can't see a damn thing beyond the chimney." I had to agree with him, the situation did look really grim. " An' I ain't got a clue as to where we are," he continued, " 'ave you ? "

" To be quite truthful Bert," I answered, " I haven't. But we can't be far from Tilford. If we can get to the pub there, we can pull in for the night. There's plenty of room for both engines on their forecourt."

" Arh," replied Bert, then after a long pause he continued, " An' I'll 'ave to pick up water somewhere guv'ner, soon."

" Well," said I, " When you are ready to move on again I'll get " Ratty " Barnett to guide you with a hurricane lantern, and when we get to the river bridge, just outside Tilford, we can both fill up there."

"Arh," drawled Bert again. This time it savoured strongly of doubt.

A hurricane lantern was produced and Ratty walked in front of the Burrell traction. Bert, with the engine in low gear, now driving and steering himself, followed the waving light. I in turn followed the red light at the rear of Bert's train, not daring to be more than a yard or so from it lest I lost sight of it in the fog. So the procession went on at about one mile an hour for forty five minutes or more.

Watching the red lamp in front of me for so long seemed to have an hypnotic effect upon me. One moment it was as big as a barn door, the next it had disappeared. Suddenly it became very clear, and dangerously close. I snapped the regulator shut, jabbing my foot down on the flywheel brake pedal at the same time, and came to a shuddering stop within two or three inches of the rear end of the Clayton portable engine at the end of Bert's train.

As the ring of the wagon's gears stopped, I heard shouting coming from up ahead of me and recognised Bert's voice. " What the 'ells happened ? " followed by, " Where are you with that — light ? "

Wondering what had gone amiss I stepped warily down from the Clayton wagon and felt my way through dense fog along the side of Bert's train. On reaching the engine, I could not see what had happened. In the hazy light shed by the headlamps of the Burrell it seemed to me that she was down by the head, but my further passage forward to discover why, was blocked by a piece of white painted timber.

Bert had now ceased his shouting and was busily engaged in getting the injector working, to bring the level of water in the boiler high enough to save the fusible plug from melting. I, meanwhile, fully convinced that the front axle of the Burrell had broken, groped around in the darkness and fog to get conclusive evidence of this.

Satisfied that he had enough water in the boiler, Bert had now joined me in my investigation. As he did so a cry of " Help " came out of the darkness somewhere to our left, followed by, " For Gawd's sake somebody show a —— light." It was the voice of Ratty.

" Where the 'ell are you ? " called Bert.

" Down 'ere in the water," came Ratty's reply.

Bert held the lantern he was carrying, high above his head, though as far as we were concerned, we could see nothing but a ring of fog, like a halo. The sound of splashing grew louder, and eventually the face of the half-drowned Ratty loomed up from over the edge of the bridge in the opaque light shed by the lantern. Except that he wore no crown, he might easily have been mistaken for Father Neptune, his bedraggled hair hanging over his eyes, his cap missing, water streaming from his clothes, and long pieces of water weed hanging from his shoulders.

It was while we were dragging Ratty from the stream that the cause of the trouble became apparent. It proved that we had reached the bridge we had been looking for, earlier than we had anticipated, the approach to it being by a very sharp bend in the road. Ratty, holding his lantern high, walking backwards to guide Bert over, had backed into the railings that guarded the edge, the impact of which sent him flying over backwards into the water a few feet below, taking with him the lantern as well.

With the sudden disappearance of the light, Bert was lost, then before he could stop the engine his righthand front wheel had broken through the railings, and dropped over the edge of the bridge, the axle coming to rest on the one brick high parapet.

By now the whole of the mill gang, who had been riding in the two living vans, had joined us. Two of them were given a lantern each and stationed one at either end of the train to warn any other traffic that might be on the road. Though on a night such as this, there was little chance of that.

Fortunately, plenty of tools and timbers were available from the mill equipment to enable us to jack the front of the Burrell up until the wheel was clear of the parapet of the bridge. Then with a large timber-jack under the front coupling we were able to strike the Burrell over inch by inch until both front wheels were firmly on the road once more.

Somewhere in the distance I heard a church clock strike three as the jacks and timbers were being replaced in the body of the Clayton wagon. Meanwhile, Den Wells, one of the mill sawyers had brewed a " dixie " of tea which he handed round in mugs to all of us. Though extremely tired and weary we had to go on our way, but as far as I was concerned I could have fallen asleep still standing up. Another of the mill staff took over Ratty's job of guiding us with a lantern, while he sat by a fire in the living van drying himself out.

After both engines had filled their tanks with water from the stream and we had started to move slowly away, I heard Bill Standen, one of the mill fellows, who was standing by the open door of the living van trailing behind the Clayton wagon, start to sing in a strong bass-baritone voice, " The old Rustic Bridge by the Mill." A lump came into my throat, and I felt proud to be able to work with men who could see the humorous side in circumstances such as this night had provided.

Within the hour we had reached the village of Tilford and our pull off for the night, or rather, what was left of it. A brief respite, and we were on our way with the dawn for home.

I thought many times of what Bert Ewings said to me that day,—" November ain't my idear of the time o' year to shift saw' tackle." and how fully I agreed with him . . .

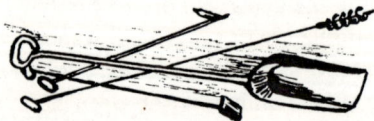

18

The Blackwall tunnel affair

" I WONDER what the Timber Merchants will do with all the cord-wood from the trees we have cut in Sidney Wood ? " mused Cyril, picking up the cube calculator and returning it to the office shelf.

" The Lord only knows," I answered, handing him the bundle of sawyers' time sheets that we had been dealing with that evening in the office. " According to my reckoning there must be well over a thousand cord lying there, to say nothing of the slab off-cuts from the mill."

This question was answered for us some fortnight later by a visit to our office of the Manager of the Timber Merchants for whom we were doing the sawmilling at Sidney Wood with a three bench mill.

" We have found a market for the cord-wood and slab off-cuts," he told us, " but it will mean cutting it into nine inch lengths for firewood and the transport of it to London. Can you undertake this work for us ? "

" Certainly," replied Cyril.

Thus it came that Father's first steam engine, the old 6 h.p. Marshall portable, was brought out of her semi-retirement and put to work on a reduced working pressure, driving a four foot circular saw, to cut the firewood. It was my ill-luck to cart the darn stuff to London with the No. 2 Clayton wagon and trailer.

" Now," said Cyril to me one day as I drove into the yard with the wagon, " there's a pile of firelogs ready for dispatch and the address is Horseferry Road, London. So tomorrow morning get

111

the wagon ready for the journey, then load up the logs in the after-noon and away first thing the next day. Your best route is straight up the main London Road to Westminster Bridge, and Horseferry Road is just over the bridge."

"It's just as easy as kissing the back of my own neck," I said, addressing Tiny, my fireman.

"It's just over forty miles each way," continued Cyril, ignoring the tone of sarcasm in my voice, "so if you leave early in the morning you should be back between 9 and 10 in the evening. When you return, Bert Bunce will take the wagon to Sidney Wood, load her with logs, return to the yard, bunker her with coal and water, and leave everything ready for you to get away early the following morning."

Now to calculate a timetable like this in the office is one thing, but to carry it out on the road is quite another. Determined to do our best, we loaded the wagon with firelogs in the afternnon and left for London just after five the next morning.

It was not long before the time schedule started to go awry ; what with not knowing my way beyond Putney, frequently taking wrong turnings, running short of water, and having not the least idea of where I could refill the tank. This last mentioned crisis quite often necessitated my breaking the law, by thieving water from horse troughs, fire-hydrants, and for the first time in my steam driving life, from a flushing valve in a public lavatory. My guardian angel must have been watching over me for I was never caught.

After many anxious moments, taking wrong roads, narrow squeaks with tram cars and a host of other uncomfortable little hazards, Horseferry Road was eventually reached. The run home was equally hair-raising but at last the sanctuary of our yard was reached and my first experience of driving in London was over, not at 9 to 10 p.m. on the day of leaving, but at 3.30 p.m. the following day. Mercifully Cyril, unlike father, had driven an engine himself and fully understood all that a stranger had to learn about driving in London. He never complained about the time I had taken but said encouragingly, " Ah well ! You'll find it a lot easier next trip "

However, before the next run was undertaken, the Road Loco-motive Users Association's advice was asked for. With their re-routing, together with a list of places where one could obtain water, the second and subsequent journeys were much easier and ran more or less to schedule.

Then came a contract to carry military hutment and steel work from a depot in Canning Town to Crawley, in Sussex. This, then, meant loading with fire-logs to Horseferry Road, running empty across London, down Commercial Road, through to Canning Town here to load with army hutment, and away through Blackwall Tunnel, Catford, Sydenham, Croydon to Crawley, the time limit now being extended to two and a half days.

My experience of the first Canning Town run is one I'll never forget. Tiny Hardman, my fireman for many months past, had now been promoted to driver, and had taken over our Clayton wagon No. 1, while Sam Barton, No. 1's old driver, at his own request had taken over the Burrell tractor, which now spent the greater part of her working life on furniture removals. I meanwhile was left to break in a new fireman, Harry Cover by name. Harry was a very likeable chap, and well versed in the art of keeping steam and water, but he hadn't ingenuity and audacity which helped so much when in a troublesome predicament.

On the new contract, the first part of the journey as far as Horseferry Road went well, but things went a little amiss when crossing the city. Now if one is really looking for excitement I can strongly recommend driving a steam wagon with a trailer behind it, up a cul-de-sac lined on both sides with market stalls, in the city of London. This is precisely what I did, and found the language of the stall holders, the would-be purchasers, and the passers-by most colourful, if not edifying.

I will not bore you with an account of how we extricated the wagon, the trailer, and ourselves unharmed; suffice it to say that we did, and arrived eventually at Canning Town. Here we were loaded by a steam crane and, by the time the last holding-down rope had been made fast, dusk had fallen.

" Ah well ! " I said to Harry, as I finished clinkering out the fire, and banked it down for the night, " that's that. Now we'll go and find somewhere to eat and sleep."

" Amen to that with all my heart," he replied.

Upon reaching the main gates of the depot on our way out, I enquired of the Security Officer on duty if there was a cafe near at hand.

" Yes," he answered hesitatingly, " of sorts, about 200 yards up this road." We thanked him and went on our way in the direction indicated. The smell soon told us that we had reached the place, it

113

was an indescribable mixture of everything from garlic, fried onion and stale tobacco smoke, to joss-stick.

It was with trepidation and misgiving, that I pushed open the door and walked into a dimly lit passage, to be greeted by a gentleman whose parentage I assessed to be that of Chinese cum Red Indian, with a goodly sprinkling of middle Africa for good measure. Both Harry and I would have turned and fled but acute hunger and the lateness of the hour prevailed over our better judgement.

I enquired whether we could have food and was assured in sing-song Chinese pidgin English that we could, and we were led into an inner room so dimly lighted that it was difficult to locate one's seat. When, however, the eyes became accustomed to the gloom and the thick acrid haze of tobacco smoke, we found that apart from a seaman in the far corner of the room, who was too drunk to know or even care where he was anyway, we were the only white people in the very overcrowded room.

Supper was served to us, and eaten, but only with partly closed eyes and a ravenous hunger could one ignore the lack of cleanliness in the table-ware and the surroundings. When supper was almost finished, the proprietor came to us and asked if we would like a room for the night, adding " Me 'ave velly plitty vhite or black girl you like too, yes ! " This remark stunned me speechless. With only one thought in mind, that of getting to hell out of the place, and quickly at that, I made some disjointed reply to the effect that we were going out for a drink first, which we did eagerly, and never went back. How sweet the London Dock air smelled that night when once outside that dreadful place.

" What do we do now ? " asked Harry in alarm.

" After what we have just been through," I managed to gulp out, " I'm going back to the depot, and find a much healthier sleep in the tender of the Clayton wagon."

As we returned from the cafe, and turned into the main gates we were met by the security policeman again, who, after hearing our story, regretted he was not allowed by regulations to let us in for the purpose of sleeping on the engine. In the course of further conversation, he enquired, " I see the name Alfold on the side of your engine ; is that the place near Loxwood in Sussex ? "

" Yes," I answered somewhat surprised that he should know our village, " do you know it ? "

" Know it ! I'll say I do. I was born in Loxwood."

He told me his name, and when it was found that I knew some of his people, this remark flung the gates of the depot wide open.

" Why the hell didn't you tell me you wanted somewhere to sleep," he chortled, " come on in the guard room, there's beds, blankets, and a fire in there."

The next morning saw us away in the early hours, and Crawley was reached without mishap.

Four journeys were accomplished before trouble came our way again. This time it was a huge R.S.J., or steel girder, 30 feet long, 1 foot 6 inches wide, by 2 feet 6 inches deep to be taken to Crawley. At first it was decided to carry it on two swinging bolsters, one on the wagon and one on the trailer, the R.S.J. resting full length on the two. It was then discovered that the entrance to the site to which it was to be delivered was halfway down a narrow lane, with a row of cottages on either side, and with a turning into the depot too sharp for the R.S.J. to negotiate loaded in this manner. An alternative plan was then used ; that of building an oak timber bolster to carry one end of the R.S.J. over the cab of the wagon, with another across the back of the wagon to carry the other end.

This time no firewood was taken up to London, but we went straight through to Canning Town. Upon our arrival the R.S.J. was carefully loaded on to the wagon by the steam crane, so that one end of the girder hung well out over the cab, about 1 foot 6 inches above our chimney the other end trailing several feet out behind, clearing the road by only a few inches. It was then secured by chains pulled tight with bottle screws, and all made ready for an early start for Crawley in the morning.

As we approached Blackwall Tunnel mouth in the morning, a policeman stepped into the road and stopped us.

" You'll have to go under the load gauge with this one, Sonnie," he said, looking up at the R.S.J. He then beckoned us into a side road under the gauge, and we cleared it by about 9 inches.

" You're alright," he assured us, " away you go."

The run down into the tunnel mouth went well, but as we reached the first bend in the tunnel road I became aware of the very light steering of the wagon. While still running at a very good speed, pondering the reason for the light steering, suddenly, and without any further warning, the front of the Clayton shot into the air and we stopped with an almighty crashing and rending sound, with the front wheels about a foot off the road.

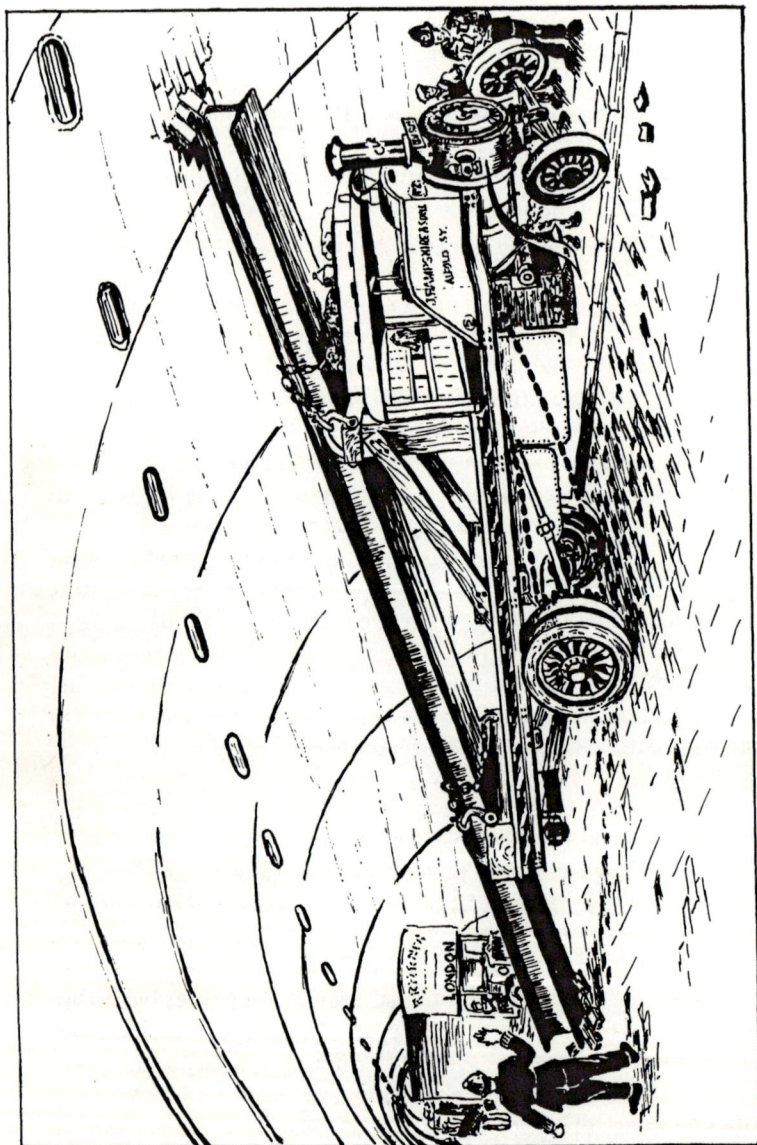

We make ourselves most unpopular in the Blackwall Tunnel. (*Drawing by the author*).

Upon examination it was found that the R.S.J. had slipped backwards to the point of balance, with the result that the front of it had jammed into the tiled ceiling of the tunnel, and the rear had dug hard into the wood paving blocks of the road. So there we were, suspended in mid air, unable to move forward or back.

It was then that I discovered that the quickest way to cause a riot was to block the traffic going in one direction through Blackwall Tunnel. The shouting, swearing, blowing of horns and the sounding of Klaxons was terriffic. Before one had time to get used to the hullabaloo however, the police were on the scene. I think they must have come from holes in the wall of the tunnel, for they were there within seconds of our enforced stop. Questions were asked, measurements were taken, the policemen wearing the most frighteningly sombre expressions as they applied their pencils to note books, giving the impression that I had deliberately sabotaged the smooth working of the tunnel, and the whole of London's traffic.

How the news of the jam up reached the far end of the tunnel I don't know, but within five or six minutes a breakdown gang arrived with huge jacks, chains, ropes, and a mobile crane. Until then the north bound traffic continued to move, but when the crane went into action, everything stopped, including my heart (or so I thought). For when a chain had been fixed to the front end of the R.S.J. and the crane pulled it down clear of the roof, the Clayton came back on to the road again with such a crash that I had grave fear of the front axle, the axle perch bracket, the smoke box, or perhaps to all three. Thank Heaven my fears were unfounded, for all were found to be unharmed.

Then came the difficulty of moving the R.S.J. back to its original position on the wagon. The crane could not relinquish its downward pull or the whole lot would have shot back up to the roof again, causing more damage to the roof tiles than had already been done. Two large foot-claw jacks were then produced and with these the back end of the girder was held up, while the crane changed over from the " pull down " to the " hoist " and in this way it was held up, a few inches clear of the bolsters. At this point the wagon was eased back under it until the marked centre point of equilibrium was reached. It was then gently lowered into position again on to the bolsters and the holding chains were replaced, but this time in such a manner as to prevent further slipping backward. One more check on the holding chains, one more thorough eaxmination of the front axle, a few more notes made in the coppers' note books, and we were away toward the south end of the tunnel and Crawley.

Apart from a little argument with a tram-car driver in Croydon as to who had the right of way, and who had the best flow of language to prove it, all went according to plan as far as Crawley.

Here we were met at the gates of the depot by a dozen or more army personnel ranging from officers and N.C.O.'s to privates, all offering advice at the same time as how best to negotiate the sharp turn in to the Depot which, as I have said before, was flanked on all sides by small cottages. Every one of them stood in front of the wagon, beckoning me in, but not one thought of the black end until halfway through the turn there came a fearful rending sound accompanied by the tinkle of falling glass, followed by a cloud of dust.

No one seemed to heed the crashing sound, but continued to beckon me on. Once inside the gates everyone, including myself, walked outside again to find out what had happened. We were confronted with a pile of brick rubble and a dear little old lady, with a command of the English language almost an a par with our own, standing amidst the wreckage holding a canary in a cage, which she had just rescued unharmed.

" Well," said the officer-in-charge, " it's about time the damned place was removed anyway." But the dear little old lady had other ideas on the matter, and names and addresses were taken again.

The trouble was caused by the end of the R.S.J. trailing out behind, and in the short turn into the gates, sweeping away the bay window of the little old lady's cottage, with the foregoing calamitous result.

The R.S.J. was eventually lifted off by a crane, and the journey back to our yard was so uneventfully quiet I felt it could not be true. But when Cyril was given a full account of the chapter of accidents that had befallen us, the remarks he passed about some of them gave me the impression that he was not overjoyed with our efforts of the past three days. Especially when the day of reckoning was over in the Law Courts ! What with the number of offences I had committed in Blackwall Tunnel, the repairs to the tunnel roof, roadway, and the costs of the breakdown gang, together with the restoration of the bay window at Crawley, I have the idea that we did not a make profit on that job at all. On the other hand though, I have a wonderful memory of Blackwall Tunnel to keep . . .

118

19

That ten day journey

WHEN FRED BROCK the driver of our 8 h.p. Burrell road locomotive took that week off to bury his grandmother, at least that's
what he said it was for, it started off a train of events that still live in
my memory.

This locomotive came into our possession when only three
or four months old. In very fact she could not even be classified as
shop soiled. She was a double crank compound, fitted with three
speed gears, two injectors, differential lock, roping drum, an extra
large capacity water belly tank, a three-quarter length cab, and a
working pressure of 200 lbs., We bought her for heavy haulage work,
but more often than not she was called upon to haul three pantechnicons for various removal firms in our nearby towns. In truth, most
of her early life with us was spent doing this. In those far-off days of
which I write, many country houses and mansions, quite understandably, preferred their household goods to be moved in one lot,
rather than by two, three, or more journeys with a steam wagon. So
it came about that when Fred took that week off it fell to my lot to
take over the Burrell road locomotive. Not that I had any objection to
that, quite the reverse, I was delighted.

A request had been received from Wyatt and Co., a firm of
removers in Guildford, for our road locomotive to haul three of their
furniture vans conveying the entire contents of a large mansion in
Worthing, to Wilton Crescent, London.

On work such as this it was the agreed practice for the removal contractors to send two professional packers with the vans ; a plentiful supply of packing material, and a number of wooden cases for the packing of china and glass. We in our turn would provide two men as assistant packers, who would also act as steersmen on the engine; the engine driver who would be in charge of the train, and a second driver to act as relief driver cum general handiman. The object of all this being that once the train was on the road it could be driven day and night throughout the journey.

By skilful contriving on the part of the packers it was somehow made possible to leave enough space in the rear van for those off duty to sleep, usually by curling themselves up in the spare soft packing or, if you were lucky, upon mattresses belonging to the servants' quarters. The head driver, while the loading or unloading was in progress, did nothing but attend to his engine; clean, polish, make any adjustment where necessary or do any minor repair. He would of course, lend a hand to help lift something heavy if required, but the efficient running of his engine was his first consideration.

Each man would take with him sufficient food to last him a week, after which he would buy his own, or, contribute to the communal food fund controlled usually by the relief driver. Carrying space for food and spare clothing was provided in a box fixed to the " Bellybox " under the rear van.

Two days before the Worthing-London journey was due to begin my brother Cyril called me to the office to be briefed. " Tomorrow," he began, " you will take the Burrell to Guildford to get the three pantechnicons and Wyatt's two packers, and bring them back here to the yard. On Saturday, Charlie Parsons and Bill Howick (our packers cum steersmen) will load $\frac{3}{4}$ of a ton of coal into each bellybox, with tools, oil, and cotton waste in the front carrier box. Meanwhile, you and Len Buxton, who will be your relief driver, will clean and prepare the Burrell ready for leaving. I'll be in the yard early on Monday morning to give you final instructions." He looked at me and smiled, "Alright ? " I nodded assent and walked from the office into the yard to confer with Len who was already busy polishing the brass and steel-work on the Burrell. Though I had driven her many times, she never ceased to fascinate me. Whenever I came near to her I would give her an affectionate pat. Len saw me do it on this occasion and gave me a very understanding smile. I'm sure he loved her as much as I did.

Saturday morning came and by 7.30 a.m. we were on our way

The author in the saddle of a 1916 Sunbeam, oilbath, 3½ h.p., 3-speed, chain drive. Behind him is a Clayton & Shuttleworth 10 h.p. double cylinder portable mill engine.

Above: Foden steam wagon, No. 13716, six-ton, three-way tipper, built 1930, rescued by the author from a scrap yard in Ely. **Below:** The same wagon, after " treatment," on a rally field in 1965. (See pp. 147-152).

to Guildford to collect the three furniture vans. All went so well on the journey that we were back in the yard again just three hours later. Soon all were busy preparing for an early getaway on Monday morning. Coal, engine stores, tools, red and white hurricane lanterns, carbide for the head lamps, and paraffin were stowed away in their respective compartments. Last of all came a box containing green baize aprons for the packers and clean overalls for the drivers.

At 6.45 on Monday we were ready and waiting for Cyril to give us our final instructions. Eventually he arrived pulling a large envelope from his pocket which he handed to me, saying, " There's fifteen pounds in there." This was for emergency use such as buying coal en route or handing out a " Sub " on the wages of any member of the crew if he required it. " I've allowed twelve days for this job," he continued, " but you should do it easily in ten. There's a drink for all of you if you're back on time. Oh, by the way," he added looking at me, " The pick-up and delivery addresses are in the envelope. So, on your way little brother, and don't waste time hanging about." My reply to this last statement was a well aimed piece of oily cotton waste that hit him squarely in the face. He made a rude gesticulation, then waved us away, shouting, " Good luck."

I gave the regulator a gentle push and pulled slowly out of the yard on to the main road. When the train was clear of the yard gates I stopped to change the engine into top gear, then waited for the " all clear " from the crew riding in the rear van through the communication cord to the gong in the engine cab. Within a brief space of time after it had sounded we were heading for Worthing at a good 7 to 8 miles an hour.

It was a beautiful morning in early March and, as we turned to the south, the sun, now just clear of the horizon, glinted on the steel link motion and connecting rods as they rocked in rhythm with the rolling crankshaft, reflecting sparkles of light upon the polished brass lubricators. Little wonder that my heart sang in harmony with the ring of the gears that morning.

Upon reaching the drive leading to the house at Worthing the vans were uncoupled. One at a time they were then pushed backwards, by hitching the drawbar to the front coupling of the engine, to the front of the house and left side by side with their tailboards facing the front door. When this had been completed Wyatt's representative handed me an inventory of all the goods in the house. Every

The Burrell and her train on the road. (*Drawing by Miss A. Child and the author*).

room and article in it had been numbered and, opposite the article was shown the number of the room to which it was to be delivered.

The task of baling up carpets, taking down pictures, packing china, glass, silverware and soft furnishings into the cases we had brought with us, began now in earnest under the watchful eye of the butler. He stayed with us until the last piece had been stowed in the vans, which had taken us four days to complete. At seven o'clock on the morning of the fifth day we headed for London.

Len and I had agreed a driving rota. I was to take the first spell, with Bill Howick as steersman, and drive as far as Beare Green. Len would then take over with Charlie as his mate as far as Esher. From here Len and I would drive and steer for each other to the end of the journey.

By the time Len had reached Esher dusk was falling. Between us the side lamps and one of the acetylene head lamps were lit, also the little oil lamp that illuminated the Klinger boiler water gauge. Meanwhile, one of the packers tended the rear light. As Len took his seat at the steering wheel I turned to him saying, " With a bit of luck, mate, I reckon we should run into Knightsbridge and Wilton Crescent between one and two in the morning." He stuck up his thumb and smiled broadly, as he said " Let her spin guv'ner." But things did not work out for us just like that.

I had been driving for some twenty minutes when patches of mist began to appear, and by the time we had reached Kingston it closed down around us like a blanket. I stopped the engine, Len then jumped down and walked round to the front of the smokebox, and extinguished the gas head-lamp. This improved our vision a little, and we trundled on again at about half a mile an hour. Having now reached Kingston Hill Len was trying his best to follow the kerb stones. Suddenly the engine gave a sideways lurch, followed immediately by an upward jump that nearly dislodged Len from his seat as the steering wheel spun out of his grip. Snapping the regulator shut and yanking the reverse lever back stopped the engine almost instantaneously. Peering down between the flywheel and the side motion cover I saw that the front wheel had mounted the kerb. A second look revealed the awful fact that the Burrell's smoke box was only inches from a large castiron pillar that carried the overhead electric tram wires. Hoping to get out of this predicament before some authority saw us, I pulled the reverse lever back and gave the auxiliary button a push. The engine moved slowly backward and the front wheel came back on to the road with a crunch and a bang.

While Len and I discussed the fog and the situation in general a policeman came walking along the pavement, " Hello," he greeted us cheerily, " Got trouble, mate ? "

" No," I answered dejectedly, " only this confounded fog."

" How far are you going with this little lot," he enquired, running his eyes along the train, the end of which was obscured from his vision by the fog.

" Close to Knightsbridge if we have any luck, but not tonight in this blasted weather."

After a brief conversation with him about the length of our train, I asked if there was a place nearby where we could pull off the road for the night. He stroked his chin thoughtfully before he spoke in reply. " Yes," he drawled, " There's a big contractor's yard about 250 yards up the hill, you'd be able to get in there. Try 'em, mate," adding finally, " They don't close till 9.30."

Len and I climbed onto the engine again, bade the officer a very good night and drove slowly through the murk to the contractor's yard. Upon reaching it, I stepped down from the fooplate and found my way to the yard foreman's office. It was with relief I learned that for a payment of two shillings we could stay there for the night. But unfortunately he could not authorise our sleeping in the van. Only too thankful to find accommodation for the train, I accepted the conditions.

" Ah well," sighed Len, " Can't be 'elped guv'ner. You drive her in and I'll walk in front to guide you. While you're banking her down I'll go and break the news to the rest of the lads."

While I was working on the engine Bill Howick came up to me saying. " There's a pub over the road, guv'ner, when you're ready we'll go over, per'a'ps the landlord can help us." A few minutes later six tired men walked into the bar, only to be told by the landlord that he could not help us. Quickly we drained our drinks and walked outside to try our luck elsewhere, Wyatt's men going one way and we four another.

Our quest for lodgings proved hopeless. After what seemed hours trudging through the fog Len suddenly stopped, " Blast this," he blurted venomously, " I'm going back to that yard and try to get in."

" And I'm right with you," said I.

The four of us then turned about and groped our way back. Finding the gates now closed and locked, and about 6 foot 6 inches in height, they presented a formidable barrier to a night's sleep.

" I've got it," announced Charilie, stepping toward the gates, " I'm the smallest of you all, I'll bend down in front of the gates, then, one at a time, climb onto my back and haul yourself to the top of the gate. When you're all up there you can pull me up." It seemed such a good idea, we put it into practice immediately. I went first and sat astride the gate, then Bill Howick followed me. Just as Len Buxton was about to pull himself up a light was flashed upon us.

" 'An' what the 'ell goes on 'ere ? " said a harsh stern voice. I peered down from the top of the gate to see who it was who could so rudely interrupt the proceedings. " Blimey," whispered Bill, " It's a couple of coppers." As truly I saw for myself, it was a sergeant of police and a constable. " Come down 'ere and let's have a look at you," continued the voice. Bill and I obeyed the command and slid from the top of the gate to the pavement.

" Who are you, where d'you come from, an' what the 'ell were you a doin' of climbing the gates ? Eh ? " asked the sergeant, all in one breath.

The four of us said our little piece in turn, describing the sad events of the evening. I produced my driving licence to prove my identity. " That don't prove anything," he grunted, and then adopting a more sinister tone said, " I'm takin' you all in so's I can get a better look at you." There seemed nothing else for it but for the four of us follow him to the police station.

Once inside we were asked a thousand questions. " Look," I said in exasperation, " Why don't you telephone my people at home, they will confirm my integrity." But no, he seemed bent on charging us with " breaking and entering." At last he submitted to telephoning Cyril, dragging him from his bed to answer it, and was finally convinced that we were not a gang of rough-necks. Although on second thoughts, in our bedraggled state he may have had some justification in thinking so. " Well," I asked, with a touch of sarcasm, " What are you going to do about it ? It's now turned midnight, we have nowhere to sleep, and we can't get into that yard."

He lifted his helmet and scratched his head, muttered " UMM," several times. Then with some reluctance said " Well, I suppose you could sleep in one of the cells." And that is precisely where we spent what was left of the night, but not locked in.

At five o'clock the next morning we were awakened by the constable on duty and given a cup of tea, after which we hurriedly made our way back to the engine. The fog having now dispersed, preparations were made to move on to Wilton Crescent. While Len climbed on to the running board to remove the chimney damper, I levelled out the fire which had been banked up the night before. At this moment Wyatt's two packers walked into the yard. Upon enquiry, they too had not found lodgings, but had walked the streets all night, though they had breakfasted at a cabmen's shelter. This reminded me that we had not eaten. Rashers of bacon and bread were brought from the food box, and soon I was busily engaged cooking the rashers in the firebox, using the clinker shovel—-the engineman's frying pan.

Since the fog and our frolics of the night before had upset our time table it became imperative that we should get to our destination as quickly as possible. Pulling out of the Kingston yard and heading for Putney Heath, with a train of our length, caused pandemonium royal to break out, as we held up the early morning workmen's tram-cars, thereby causing unprintable caustic remarks to be hurled in both directions by all drivers concerned. Despite where the tram drivers told us to take our train, we arrived safely on Putney Heath. Here I planned to lay by until early evening, before making the attempt to get through Wimbledon. The law frowned severely upon road locomotives, especially with a train like we had, using certain roads and streets in Central London between the hours of 10 p.m. and 6 a.m. I therefore planned to get through Wimbledon and to reach the outskirts of Knightsbridge within the approved hours. And, believe me, you were not welcomed even within those hours.

Although the speed limit of a heavy road locomotive in country areas was four miles an hour, in towns it was cut to two. But my experience, and I think that of other drivers too, was that you could drive like the clappers of hell in London, for if a policeman saw you he declined to do anything about it. I think he was only too delighted to see your tail-light vanish out of his area into that of his colleague's.

From Putney Heath all went as scheduled, and as we drove into Wilton Crescent that night, Big Ben boomed out the hour of twelve-thirty.

Leaving Len to " bed down " the engine, I went to the house

to report our arrival and to arrange for an early start in the morning for nuloading. The few staff that were there were overjoyed to see me, since they had nothing in the house in the way of furniture for their use.

Although the next day was a Sunday, the process of unloading went on as usual, but to mark the Sabbath we were all called to the kitchen, where the butler read to us a short passage from the New Testament, and a prayer was said for the well being of all. Within minutes we were back to work again. Carpets, where possible, were laid; pictures hung where detailed and packing cases emptied. This time all orders were given by the housekeeper, and in no uncertain manner. Even the old butler was subdued in her awesome presence.

All through Sunday the work went smoothly on, but on Monday morning a telegram from home was handed to me—requesting me, when empty, to drive to Chalfont St. Peter, and stating that money and orders awaited me at the post office there. " Aw blimey, here we go again," groaned Len as I read the message to him, " Now where the 'ell do we finish up ? " " Gawd only knows," I answered dolefully, putting the missive into the box at the back of the cab of the engine. " We can only wait till we get to Chalfont to find that out." Len walked away to continue his work with the unloading, while I went back to my job of cleaning out the mechanical lubricator on the engine.

A little later Charlie came up to me. " Can you give us a hand to get this infernally heavy grand piano in, guv'nor ? " he asked. " Sure," I answered, " I'll be right with you." Charlie was right, it was heavy. It was as much as the six of us could do to lift the thing, I remembered it from loading, but at last it was in position in the room numbered to take it. Bill Howick, a humorist in his own right, then, thinking the housekeeper was out of the house opened up the keyboard, pulled up a chair and cramming a silk topper onto his head at a rakish angle proceeded to regale us with his version of " Knocked 'em in the Old Kent road." Halfway through the first chorus the door burst open and in flounced the housekeeper, and slammed down the lid of the piano nearly amputated Bill's fingers, then stormed out of the room without saying a word to anyone. " The ruddy old hag," lamented Bill, rubbing his fingers. " Tell you what," he continued, " I'll bet a quid she holds a licence to ride a flaming broom stick. She's got no sense of humour. That's what."

Just after noon on Tuesday the vans were empty, and preparations were made to leave London that night for Chalfont St. Peter. The tender and belly tanks had been filled with water, the van wheels oiled and the headlamps recharged with fresh carbide. At six o'clock the fire was lit in the engine to raise steam. While we were discussing the question of supper, one of the maids came out to us with an invitation to all for a hefty meal in the kitchen. This I learned later was due to Bill Howick's overtures to the cook. By 11.30 that night we were pulling out of Wilton Crescent in the direction of Chalfont St. Peter.

Before our departure Len and I had consulted our map, concluding our best route would be via Acton, Southall, Uxbridge and Gerrards Cross, our first consideration being that of finding water. The Burrell's normal range on tender and belly tanks was about 15 to 18 miles, according to load and hills encountered. The tender tank would be sufficient to travel about 11 miles. When this was empty, who ever was driving would open the belly tank valve to let the water there in flow into the tender tank. This would enable us to run another 5 to 7 miles, during which time the driver and steersman would be on the alert for a river, pond, stream or any other suitable place to refill the tanks. Len had agreed to take the first spell of driving with Charlie Parsons as steersman, planning to reach Hillingdon before picking up water. Upon his arrival there he was to wake me, then Bill Howick and I would take the engine on to our destination. What went wrong is not quite clear, for as Len reached a point just west of Acton the tender tank was empty. He opened the belly tank valve and warned Charlie of what he had done. Knowing now that they could only run on a few more miles, both kept an eye open for a water supply.

About a mile from Southall Len sighted a horsetrough and pulled alongside it. While Charlie uncoiled the suction hose, Len came to the rear van to wake me and explain what he was about to do. As it was illegal to take water from horse-troughs it became necessary to post one man to watch forward, while another would keep an alert eye to the rear. If either saw a policeman, he would start to whistle a tune, thus giving the driver time to turn off the water lift and pull the hose from the trough.

All was going fine, neither Charlie or I saw a copper anywhere until one suddenly appeared at Len's elbow as he stood with one hand on the lifter steam valve, ready to shut off if the warning was given.

128

"Oh! Good morning constable," said Len politely, it now being about one a.m.

"I suppose you know that what you are doing is against the law," said the constable sternly, utterly ignoring Len's polite salutation.

Len eyed the young policeman, who now stood in the full light of the street lamp over the trough. Assessing him to be only a week or so in the force, and taking a chance that his knowledge of steam might be limited, exclaimed, "Yes, sir, I know it is, but our need is real desperate, 'cause if we don't get some water into that boiler soon she's goin' to blow up. And Gawd help you and an' me if she does."

Charlie, who now stood by the tender of the engine, noting the trend of the conversation between Len and the police constable, decided to try and make the "Blow up" a little more realistic by reaching up and turning the water off from the injector that Len had left working. As the roar of steam came from the now water-starved injector he started to run, shouting as he did so, "For Gawd's sake run Len, she's goin' up."

It took Len about half a second to realize Charlie's handiwork, then he too started to run, hotly pursued by the young constable, who upon catching up with Len, panted. "If water will stop that confounded contraption from blowing up, then for heaven's sake take some and get to hell out of it," adding furtively, "But don't tell anyone you've seen me." As Len made his way back to the engine, the policeman walked in the opposite direction at quite a brisk pace.

"Good work, Charlie," said Len, laughing as they coiled up the suction hose together, "'twas a chance in a million, mate, but it worked."

I meanwhile had closed the injector steam valve, and made up the fire. As Len joined me on the footplate I told Charlie that he could have a rest, and that I would take over steering for Len. While making myself comfortable in the steersman's seat Charlie's signal came on the gong, and seconds later we were rumbling away into the night, on through Hayes, Hillingdon, Gerrards Cross to Chalfont St. Peter.

In the early hours before the dawn a misty rain developed, making everything so cold and damp that, if the damper should be fully closed, the exhaust steam from the chimney would beat down around the engine as to almost obliterate the roadside from the steers-man's vision.   At last a point was reached about half a mile from Chalfont. Here the train was brought to a standstill by the side of the road to await the coming of daylight, and the hour at which the post office would open. This well earned respite allowed two very tired men, Len and me, to make a drink of tea, by hanging the iron kettle in the firebox on the end of the poker. Teapot ? Oh dear no, just add tea, sugar and tinned milk to the boiling water in the kettle. Sergeant major's tea I think it was called ; hot and sweet.

When daylight came the train was pulled to within walking distance of the post office. Here I left Len to tend the wants of the engine while I went to collect the mail and the money that awaited me there. The instructions in the letter were for me to go to Chalfont Common, to the home of Admiral Sir John " X," and to transport the contents of the house and outside effects to an address at Row-berrow.

" Where the hell is Rowberrow," enquired Len as I read Cyril's letter to him.

" I haven't a clue," I answered truthfully, " but I expect someone at the admiral's place will be able to tell us."

We had no trouble in finding the admiral's house, and within an hour of our arrival the three vans were in position at the front of the house. Wyatt's representative had left the inventory for us, together with the money for their own two packers.

Most of the staff had already left for the new address, leaving only the cook, parlourmaid, the chauffeur and the admiral himself, who, on the whole, was an extremely nice man, except that every-thing had to be done his way, " Ship-shape and Bristol fashion, lads." he would keep saying. After being given a hearty meal at mid-day the packing of cases during the afternoon and evening went on swimmingly.

On the morning of the third day at Chalfont, having previously driven the Burrell round to the courtyard at the back of the house, I was busy washing out the boiler when Charlie shouted to me. " Come and give us a hand guv'nor." I left what I was doing and followed him to the landing on the second floor, where the rest of the gang stood contemplating a huge ornate piece of furniture. " I reckon we'll have to take it to pieces," said one. " Yes, it's the only way we'll do it," said another.   At this moment the admiral appeared on the landing. " No need for that, men," said he, authoritatively, " we'll lower it away with blocks." Then turning to his chauffeur ordered him to fetch the ropes and tackle.

" Make fast the double sheave to that 'Samson' post," ordered the admiral, pointing to the wooden column of the third floor balustrade, he then busily engaged himself knotting a rope sling round the massive piece of furniture. When all was ready he handed us the rope end of the tackle, shouting, " Haul away, men." As we did so an ominous creaking sound came from the landing above. The heavy piece of furniture swung out clear of the banister as we pulled, " Lower away, lads," the admiral sang out. Then came a dreadful rending and tearing sound from up aloft and the ornate piece went down with a run, taking with it the greater part of the third floor balustrade. All went crashing down onto the floor of the hall below, disintegrating into a hundred pieces with a noise that could well have wakened the dead. The admiral used a few-well chosen words applicable to such an occaision, then left us to our own devices. We never saw him again until we reached the house at Rowberrow.

The greatest privation one can suffer when driving a steam engine on the road for any length of time, is the lack of washing facilities ; though one can wash hands and face as often one pleases, with reservations, as time will allow on the road, by obtaining hot water from the injector in a pail. Having now been away from home for thirteen days, and not removing any of my clothes during this time, not even to sleep, I longed desperately for a bath. On the Sunday evening, the day the Admiral left us in a hurry, and the house staff had gone to their rooms at the local inn, Len and I procured an empty corn bin from the stables and carried it into the kitchen. By using pots and kettles on the kitchen range for hot water we had the most luxurious bath, even washing our shirts and underclothing, which were dried in front of the fire as we sat in just our trousers.

By nine o'clock on Tuesday morning the last piece had been loaded into the vans, a hurried meal was prepared and eaten, and just before eleven we pulled out of the drive to the main road heading for Rowberrow, some 120 miles away. Mapping our route to take us through Marlow, Reading, Newbury, Devizes, and Bath ; stopping at Devizes to pick up a ton and a half of Welsh coal, driving in four hour shifts, with the Burrell running perfectly, we pulled up at the drive gates of the admiral's new home, near Weston-Super-Mare, just 27 hours after leaving Chalfont Common.

Here our troubles started with a capital " T ". The drive gates were so narrow that it became necessary to " side chain " each van through the gates with two men steering the van by its drawbar, then coupling the three together again after they were through the gates.

When halfway up the drive, which was a mile and a quarter long, we came to an iron bridge spanning a shallow stream. Not liking its appearance, Len and I, got down from the engine to examine it more closly before attempting to cross over.

" I don't like the look of it," said Len.

" Neither do I," I replied.

The bridge appeared to be constructed of rolled steel joists about four inches deep, set in concrete on either side, with a span of roughly seven feet, and clearing the water by some fifteen inches or so. Bolted to the side R.S. joists was a runner bearing four stanchions and a hand rail, all of which was made of cast iron, while across the steel girders, to form the road, were fixed wooden railway sleepers. Just how many of the girders there were we could not see, owing to reeds and other water weeds growing there.

By now, Len and I had been joined by Charlie, Bill and Wyatt's two packers. " Hold everything," said Bill in an undertone, " It's 'is Nibs himself coming down the road."

" What is the trouble men." enquired the admiral brusquely, as he came up to us.

" I have grave doubts about the strength of this bridge, sir," I answered.

" Great heavens, man, it's built to carry twenty tons," he ejaculated, giving emphasis to the word twenty.

" That may be so, sir, but I still have qualms of it being able to take our weight."

We argued the subject for some minutes, eventually I struck a bargain with him. " Very well, sir," I spoke with an air of finality, " I will take the chance of crossing the bridge, providing you will accept all responsibility for any damage to myself, the engine, the vans or the bridge."

The admiral pondered this ultimatum for a few moments, " Very well, I will accept all liability."

At this, I returned to the engine and mounted the footplate, put the Burrell into second gear, opened the regulator and moved toward the bridge, but not without some anxiety. As the front wheels passed over I distinctly felt the tremor, but when the hind wheels approached the centre of the bridge it sagged to the extent of six inches or more. The undue strain on the cast-iron runners caused them to explode with a loud report, scattering pieces in all directions like shrapnel, one piece giving Charlie an awful clout in the side of his neck, as he stood watching the crossing. At the sound of the report I pushed the regulator wide open. With terrific " barks " from the exhaust the Burrell leapt the remaining distance across the bridge like a wounded tiger, and I made no attempt to stop until the three vans were over the bridge as well.

When I did stop the train, the rest of the crew came up thanking providence for a safe crossing, with Charlie still rubbing his neck, where the iron had hit him, and swearing with every word he knew.

" Are you hurt, Charlie ? " I enquired anxiously.

" Lor' bless you no, guv'nor, it stings a bit though."

" Pity you couldn't have seen the vans comin' over, guv'nor. They jumped in and out of that dent in the bridge like three mountain goats," said Len as he climbed to the steersman's seat.

When everyone was aboard again we drove on up the drive, pulling in front of the house as darkenss fell. There were only two of the male staff waiting for us and after conferring with them, it was decided to let them have mattresses and rugs for the night and make an early start in the morning to unload.

Unloading began with the coming of daylight, but right to the end, three days later, there was NO helpful advice from the admiral. He left us severely alone. During those three days I watched Charlie closely, and with growing anxiety, for it was obvious the fellow was far from well. In the afternoon of the third day I called Charlie to one side, " Are you sure you are feeling alright, Charlie ? " I asked. " Tomorrow we'll be leaving for home, and there's no need for you to do your spell on duty if you're not well."

" Lor' bless you guv' ! " he broke in, " I'll do my turn if I die doing it," and dismissed the whole thing with a shrug of his shoulders, but I noticed his face contort with pain as he did so.

That evening the ton of coal I had ordered to be delivered to us was stowed away in the bellyboxes, the packing material replaced in the vans, and the doors closed and barred. I enquired of the parlour maid whether I might be allowed to speak to the admiral. He came to to me in the hall. " We will be leaving in the morning, sir," I announced, " and I would like to know if there is another way out of the estate, to avoid the risk in crossing that bridge again."

" I have given that matter some thought, driver," he looked at me and smiled. " There is a way through the home farm to the highway. It's a hard road, but very muddy through the farm." He laid one hand on my shoulder and pressed a pound note into my palm with the other, saying, " Thank you, driver, and good luck on your journey."

The next morning we left the admiral's house and turned off the drive onto the farm road, through mud inches deep, eventually reaching the main road, then turned east toward Blagdon, and home, some 150 miles away via Warminster, Salisbury, Winchester and Petersfield. Although Len and I were working the four hourly shift, as usual, I would not permit Charlie to do more than one hour at a stretch, however much he protested against it.

At Frome, Len took over the Burrell with Charlie steering for his allotted hour. A few miles out of Frome, Len was busy with the fire shovel, firing up, when he felt Charlie's hand touch him on the shoulder, he turned to look up. Seeing the expression on Charlie's face he snapped the regulator of the engine shut and spun the fly-wheel brake on. As the wheels of the Burrell ceased to turn Charlie made an attempt to leave the steering seat, then slumped forward into Len's arms. " Quick, guv'nor, come quick," shouted Len at the top of his voice. I was dozing in the rear van and did not hear him call. One of Wyatt's men roused me, saying, " Len's calling you Mr. 'ampshire." I jumped from the van and ran to the engine, followed by Bill Howick, receiving a dreadful shock when I saw the state Charlie was in. Between us he was lifted from the tender of the engine and carried to the rear van where we laid him on a bed of soft packing. While I was bending over to reassure him that he would be alright, he looked at me, trying to smile, and whispered, " I'm sorry, Guv'nor." Then lapsed into unconsciousness.

" Len," I whispered, " we've got to get a doctor quickly." Then I walked into the middle of the road to stop the first vehicle that came along, it mattered not in which direction. It was an interminable time before a small van came by. I explained the position and the owner was only too pleased to help, even to driving me to three doctors, it being a Sunday, before I could find one who could come immediately. Thanking the van driver I climbed into the doctor's car and sped hastily back to the train.

Upon arrival the doctor took one look at Charlie and said, "Help me get him into my car, it's a hospital case I'm afraid." Len and I lifted the limp body of Charlie on to the back seat of the car. I seated myself by the doctor who drove like the devil to the nearest hospital, but it was all to no purpose, for on our arrival poor Charlie was dead.

The next two hours for me was a veritable nightmare of which I will not speak here. The doctor was kind enough to drive me back to the engine, where the rest of the crew were waiting for what news I could bring them. The shock was as great to them as it had been for me, especially to Len.

As we could not move from where we had stopped until the police had interviewed us, to take statements in the morning, red lanterns were lit and placed at the head and rear of the train. But none of us slept that night.

The police came out to where we were waiting at about nine o'clock on Monday, taking a statement from every man in the crew. Each in turn gave his version of the events from the breaking of the bridge, until Charlie collapsed on the engine. The police then warned me that Len and I would be called to give evidence at the Coroner's inquest. It was nearly 11 o'clock before we were left to continue our journey home. A journey that remains vividly in my memory, for Charlie's death and the simple events that led up to it, had been a great shock to us all.

Len and I tried to work our four-hour rota, but now being one man short it necessitated overlapping the time by steering for each other, to enable Bill to have his rest. Wearily all through Monday night and Tuesday we travelled on in the direction of home, with scarcely a word spoken between us. On Wednesday morning, with heavy hearts, we pulled into our yard, just twenty-four days after leaving it.

The twenty-four day trip as related, transpired to be the last but one furniture job the Burrell did. The quickly changing methods of transport were, alas, surely pushing the road locomotive with its three vans off the roads, and we had to change with the times. But our big Burrell continued on, engaged on the work we intended her for—heavy haulage. Of one thing I am eternally grateful, that of the honour of driving one of these big engines while they were still the " Monarchs of the Road."

As a post script. The doctor's evidence at the coroner's

inquest in simple language was, that the blow Charlie had received so damaged the jugular vein in the neck as to finally stop the flow of blood to the brain . . .

20

Disaster follows disaster

OLD JOE BARNETT had been out of hospital about six weeks when the Newlands Corner timber job was started Joe had been one of our best sawyers until he had an argument with a six foot circular saw and lost the first three fingers of his right hand, but it took more than the loss of a few fingers to put Joe out of action, for he could do as much with his thumb and little finger as most people could do with a complete hand. He wanted so much to go back to the sawmill to work, but Cyril thought it far better for him to have a change of work. So, he was now acting as my mate on our old 6 h.p. Burrell traction engine, hauling timber from the Warren, in the Surrey Hills, to an open space at Newlands Corner where it would be stacked for re-loading later.

To get from Newlands Corner to the Warren we had to travel along the top of the Surrey Hills for about two miles on the old " Pilgrims Way " in the direction of Dorking. Then we turned off to the left down a still rougher track into a vast pine forest known as the Warren. Here hundreds of trees had been felled the winter before and now had to be hauled out to the main road, re-loaded on to other transport and taken to Guildford station. There they would be loaded into rail wagons and consigned to Woolwich to be made into telegraph poles.

For the carriage of the timber from Newlands Corner to Guildford we had our Clayton Wagon No. 2 with bolsters and trailer, and Burrell 5 ton tractor with a timber carriage.

My part in the operation was to rope the trees into a lump, load them on to a timber carriage, then haul them from the Warren to the main road. Here they would be unloaded and made into a pile under a crane, which would later re-load them on to the Clayton wagon, or the timber carriage of the Burrell tractor, as and when each returned from Guildford.

Since there was no water to be had anywhere along our route, or in the Warren, it became necessary to take with us each day a tractor trailer to which had been fitted a 500 gallon tank, holding sufficient water for the engine's use for one day. This water trailer would be coupled to the end of the timber carriage pole, taken in with us, then left in the pine wood until the evening. Three or four journeys a day would be made to the main road with timber, and on the last journey the water trailer would be taken out. At our unloading point stood a traction engine truck with an 800 gallon water tank fitted to it. This was for the Clayton wagon and the Burrell tractor's use.

Each evening both trucks would be coupled behind the Burrell traction and taken down the main road to the foot of the hill toward Gomshall, where the tanks would be filled with water taken from the historic " Silent Pool." For this purpose we had fitted up an old Model " T " Ford engine to drive a 2 inch rotary pump. It was a far from handsome effort, but it worked well and that was all we asked of it. When both tanks were full they would be taken back up the hill to our camp, and left ready for use the next day.

Sleeping accommodation for the gang was two six-berth living vans, left side by side close by the piled timber, about a hundred yards from the main Dorking, Merrow and Guildford road, affording the most spectacular view from the van doors, right across the counties of Surrey and Sussex to the sea, beyond the Sussex Downs, thirty to thirty-five miles away.

The whole crew on the job consisted of: Joe and his brother " Ratty " Barnett, who worked with me on the old Burrell traction, Tiny Hardman and Jack Edwards on the Clayton wagon, " Jacko " Mills and Bob Burstow on the Burrell tractor. As I remember them, they were a happy-go-lucky gang never uttering an angry word, and not one cared whether he worked eight hours a day, or fifteen, more often than not it was the latter number.

Some of my readers may remember the summer of 1921, or if not, most probably will have heard of it. It was the hottest summer

I ever knew. Not a spot of rain fell in our area for over thirteen weeks and loading timber down in the hollow of the Warren in such conditions was worse than working in an oven. It was bad enough working on the footplate of the old Burrell, I could at least wear the barest of clothing and canvas shoes, but Joe and Ratty dared not dispense with boots and leggings because of the number of adders encountered. They were, in, on, and under practically every tree. To use Ratty's expression, " The damn place was lousy with 'em," and he should know for he was bitten twice during the two months we were there, but being real countrymen, both he and Joe always carried with them an antidote for snake bites, made and given to them, so they told me, by an old gypsy who lived nearby.

Great though my loathing of snakes, my biggest worry when moving about was that of rabbit holes and tree stumps, Since the Warren from end to end was covered with heather and bracken almost knee high. it obscured both these obstacles from view. So that each time I had to move the engine to get another angle of pull with the wire rope, I would run foul of one or the other, or both. If it was a rabbit hole, then, invariably the engine would sink into the sandy earth and come to rest on her tender tank, bringing with it all the extra work of extricating her from the hole. This particular form of trouble would come my way, at very least, once a day.

Another problem too, was that of pulling out of the Warren up the steep slope to the Pilgrims Way with a heavy load, without setting fire to the forest with sparks from the chimney. Despite the use of spark arresters, one fitted in the smokebox and one up the chimney, it was a very real hazard and beater brooms were carried with us, as well as being stacked at frequent intervals along the route, to deal with an out-break.

Apart from the spinning whirligig of chance referred to above, life for the first fortnight of the job went on smoothly. Until the early hours of one morning when we were all rudely awakened by someone banging loudly on the open doors of the van where Joe and three others were sleeping. .

" Sorry to disturb you, lads," said a powerful voice, " We are police officers, and would like a word with you."

" An' you picked a —— fine time of the mornin' t'do it too, ahn't ee'." I heard Joe shout from his bunk, " It's quarter t' three," he continued, " What th 'ell d' you want ? "

By now the inmates of both vans were really wide awake

and most of them swearing lustily at being disturbed at that unearthly hour.

" We would like to ask you what you know about the car that stands by your vans," replied one of the plain clothes policemen.

" Well it ain't mine." " Nor mine," we shouted in chorus. The questions that then followed from the police spokesman baffled us completely. After an hour of interrogation we were left alone, still none the wiser as to what it was all about. And, not until Tiny returned with the Clayton from Guildford, after delivering his first load the next morning did we get some inkling. " Some damned authoress has disappeared," he announced, " And that's her confounded car standin' there. It's all in the papers this morning. Here you are guv'nor," he said handing me the paper, "read it to 'em." I took it from him and read the headlines to the rest of the gang standing round me.

" An' flaming good luck to 'er," said Bob Burstow as I finished reading, " All I 'ope is she 'ad as much aleep as we did last night." Everyone agreed with Bob's sentiments, and the whole thing was dismissed from our minds. But unfortunately we were not allowed to forget it for long. For the greater part of a fortnight we were pestered daily by detectives asking numerous and, to us, inane questions to which none of us knew the answers.

Then came shock number one. Three detectives arrived one evening and asked us to submit to our finger prints being taken. Feeling quite sure that none of our fellows were guilty of any crime, I suggested they gave in to it, and relieved the suspense by allowing mine to be taken first. Joe then caused a little diversion by holding up his right hand, with the fingers missing, saying, " I' low as you'll 'ave some job takin' mine, mate." The following evening came shock number two. The same " tecs " arrived, and called me aside. They informed me that they were about to take Tiny's mate, Jack Edwards in for further questioning as number one suspect. Jack was called over and asked about his fingerptints on the car. It seems that when the authoress abandoned her car she left one door open, and Jack seeing it thus, thinking he was doing someone a good turn, closed it, thereby leaving his fingerprints on the handle, which were found by the police, but not having sufficient evidence for his arrest, Jack was allowed to remain with us.

The next morning came the news that the authoress had

declared her where-abouts, in France I think it was, just in time to save Jack from being arrested. The whole thing, as far as it involved us, died a natural death. We were left to continue our work un-molested that is, as far as the police were concerned, but the oppressive-heat, rabbit holes and adders remained very much with us.

For a few days now things had been going so smoothly I began to wonder whether it might prove to be the lull before the storm, and foolishly said as much to old Joe.

" Arh," drawled Joe in his broad Sussex dialect, " I 'low as we'll atter suffer fer this afore long, mark my words. 'Tis all gwain too smooth like, t' last."

That evening as we coupled up the two trucks with the water tanks on and went down to the Silent Pool to fill them, Joe's pro-phecy was fulfilled. When both tanks were full I backed the old Burrell to the trucks, Joe dropped the coupling pin into place, and climbed on to the engine to steer for me. Ratty, meanwhile, took his seat on the rear truck and the long drag up the steep winding hill to our camp began. For short journeys such as this, we had dispensed with the communication cord, thus, I would frequently look back through the cab stays of the Burrell for any vehicle that might want to overtake us.

We had now reached a point midway up the hill, where on my right-hand side the grassy slope of the downs rose away at a steep angle, while on my left was a two foot high bank, topped by a ten foot wide grass track. Beyond this the ground fell away in rolling downland toward the distant village of Albury. I looked back down the hill, there wasn't a car in sight, and all looked so peaceful in the late evening sun. A few seconds later something made me look back again. It couldn't have been someone shouting, for had they done so, I would never have heard it in the cab of the Burrell for the colossal din made by her gearing, which I can only liken to being in a belfry with a full peal of bells, rung out of rhythm. As I looked back my heart missed a beat at what I saw, our back truck had broken it's drawbar and was careering backward down the hill, with Ratty preparing to make a jump to get clear. It kept a straight course for some twenty yards, then veered off to climb backwards up the grassy slope. The sudden stop sent a surge of water from the tank like a tidal wave, washing Ratty from the back of the truck onto the grassy bank, unhurt but dreadfully wet. The truck then shot across the road to hit the low bank on the other side and capsized, throwing the tank bumping and rolling into the roadway with an indescribable booming.

"Arh, guv'nor," said Joe, standing with his arms akimbo looking at the wreckage, "I know'd as summat was gwain t'appen. An' now 't 'as."

It was well after one o'clock in the morning before we had got everything cleared up and back to our camp. The next morning Tiny took the broken drawbar to Guildford in the Clayton wagon to be welded. Until it was returned I was unable to resume work in the Warren, through lack of our water supply.

With the return of the repaired drawbar, the next three days passed without any untoward happenings, but, the fourth morning as Joe mounted the engine to take his seat at the steering wheel, he gave me a look that I knew and understood only too well. "Joe," I said, in mock sternness, "If you are thinking what I think you are, then keep it to yourself, I've had enough of your blasted prophecies to last me quite a while.

He settled himself in the steersman's seat, and a wry grin spread over his face as he spoke to me.

"'Twont make no dif'rence if I do, Guv'nor," he drawled, "'t 'll 'appen jus' same."

I finished firing up and dropped the shovel back into the bunker before I spoke again, "Well at five o'clock in the morning, Joe, I don't want to know anything about it." As Joe grunted something in reply I opened the old Burrell's regulator and we bumped and clanged along the Pilgrims Way to the Warren.

Our first load of timber that morning triggered off a string of troubles. We were clearing up a few odd trees left in one corner of the Warren. These now had been roped up on to the carriage and preparations were being made to move on to another pile to complete the load. While Ratty removed the skids and rolling chains, Joe coupled up the Burrell's wire rope to the carriage drawbar with the "double hooks." When Ratty was clear of the carriage, Joe gave me the signal to pull. For a few feet it ploughed smoothly through the bracken, then one hind wheel of the carriage rose up on to a tree stump, while it's mate on the opposite side sank deep into a rabbit hole. This combined action sent the loaded trees skidding to one side against the retainer pillar, with such force as to turn the rear bolster round on the carriage pole, the trees rumbled off, leaving the timber carriage turned inside out.

This catastrophe only seemed to whet the appetites of the Evil Spirits—whose sole mission on earth is to bedevil timber hauliers—to far greater efforts. At least that was Joe's version of the happenings. If this were the case, then those said devils immediately left the timber carriage to join me on the old Burrell, and bided their time to strike again.

The only way to get the carriage upright again was to move the engine square on to it, pull the tangled trees clear, then hitch the engine's wire rope to the upturned bolster and pull, with a fervent prayer that it would not break the carriage pole in the process. Threading my way cautiously through the tree stumps I brought the Burrell round to the required position. As I stopped Ratty removed the road-pin from the engine's hind wheel to free the rope drum.

" What's the ground like down there, Ratty ? " I enquired.

" No worse than anywhere else in the Warren," he answered, digging his heel into the ground as a test.

The rope was then run out and made fast to the trunks still resting on the front bolster, to pull them clear. And, not until Joe gave me the signal to gently haul away, did I become aware that the engine was taking on a pronounced list to one side. I got down from the footplate to satisfy myself that all was well before attempting to pull, and was horrified to find that the lower step on the tender was already squeezed below the surface of the ground. Ratty, and Joe must have seen the change of expression on my face, and walked over to see what was wrong. As we stood watching we could actually see the old Burrell slowly, very slowly, going over, but, what was worse, there was simply nothing we could do to prevent it from happening. My first impulse was to race for a rolling chain to fasten on, to try and keep her upright, but the nearest standing tree for a suitable anchor was at least half a mile away.

Soon she had reached an alarming angle, with a space of some six inches showing under one hind wheel. I was convinced now that inevitably she must go right over on to her side. I thought of the fire in the firebox and reached for the clinker shovel to withdraw it. Joe, seeing what I was about to do gripped my arm, saying, " Don't 'e do that, guv'nor, you'll set th 'ole forest afire." The full implication of Joe's words appalled me, for had I thrown those red hot coals down on to that sun-baked braken and heather, the conflagration it would have caused, would have been too dreadful to contemplate.

The space under the Burrell's hind wheel had now multiplied to inches and the speed of her movement increased perceptibly. A few minutes later she gave a little shudder as she came gracefully to rest in an undignified position on her side, with not even a wisp of escaping steam in protest. The whole movement from beginning to end was so slow, that when she finally touched down in the sandy soil, the only damage she did to herself was the bending of two cab stays. After doing what we could to prevent fire, we began our long trudge back, Joe and Ratty to our camp, and I to the nearest telephone to inform Cyril as to what had happened.

As we climbed out of the Warren, I looked back on the chaos below. The timber carriage lying inside out with trees scattered all around, and the Burrell on her side a few yards away made a picture the like of which I had never seen before, nor ever want to again. Viewed from my vantage point high up on the Pilgrims Way they might well have been toys dropped by a child when play was over. How those Evil Spirits of Joe's must be laughing now, I thought. I gave a side glance at Joe trudging along by my side, and concluded it wiser not to put my thoughts into words.

That evening Cyril motored up to the Warren to see for himself the general state of things. Together we agreed that our 8 h.p. Burrell road locomotive would be the greatest help to restore order from chaos. Meanwhile Joe, Ratty and I would do all we could to get things ready for the big Burrell which would come to our aid when she returned from a long haul two days hence.

It was while we were digging the earth away from the hind wheel of the old Burrell, that we discovered the reason for her sinking and finally going over. Of all the places I could have stopped to take that pull, I had to choose one that was literally undermined with rabbit holes. Such a spot Joe called " A Rabbit Bury."

In due course our big Burrell arrived with Len Buxton driving her, bringing at the same time a truck load of tools and equipment. Early the next morning a start was made to get the old Burrell up on to her wheels again, and under Cyril's direction and supervison by ten o'clock that same night she, and the timber carriage, had been pulled upright and towed back to our base at Newlands Corner. When Len first saw the old Burrell on her side, he came up to me and whispered laughingly, " You'll be looking for a new job after this little affair, guv'nor, wont you ? " He ducked and ran as I playfully made to strike him.

The following morning Cyril returned bringing with him our fitter, Bob Hooker. Together the three of us carried out a minute examination of the old Burrell. Incredible as it may seem, apart from the cab stays to which I have already referred, she had suffered no damage at all, in fact she was in steam and back at work the day following the examination.

When sufficient timber had again been hauled to the re-loading area under the crane, the Burrell tractor and the Clayton wagon returned to work.

Some week or ten days after work had been resumed in the Warren, the seven members of the gang sat by the two living vans enjoying an evening meal and a smoke. It was an evening of outstanding beauty, with the atmosphere so clear that we could see the flicker of light on the sea through the gap in the Sussex Downs. My reverie was rudely broken by Jack Edward's voice, "Blimey," he said, pointing away to the south, " somebody's having a warm up this evening." We all looked in the direction indicated, to see a column of white smoke billowing straight up into the still air.

" Wonder what's on fire ? " mused one. Several suggestions were offered, from houses to hay stacks.

" Wonder where it is ? " enquired another. " Somewhere near Cranleigh I'd say," declared Ratty, " There's the tall chimney at Baynard's brick-yard, just to the left of the smoke, look."

Suddenly the smoke turned from grey to black and rose still higher into the sky. " Where ever it is," murmured Tiny, " It's one hell of a fire." One by one each drifted back to finish his last chores of the day, and the fire was forgotten.

Some time just before noon the next day, I found Cyril waiting for me by the loading crane as I came up from the Warren with my second load that morning. He rose stiffly from where he had been sitting and walked to meet me. He looked tired and haggard, his hands were grimed and his face streaked with soot marks. " Hello," I said in greeting, disregarding his appearance and looking in the direction of a strange car, " bought a new car."

" No," he answered slowly, " but I'm afraid we will soon have to."

His weariness and tone of voice brought me to earth with a sickening thud. I looked at him anxiously, and thought of the fire we had seen the night before. " Oh my God, Cyril," I exclaimed in apprehension, " don't tell me that fire we saw——"

" Yes," he broke in, " it was our yard. I've been there all night."

He walked back to the pile of trees by the crane and sat down. For all his 6 foot 7 inches height he was a bent broken man. Slowly he related to me all that had happened. The alarm had been raised about two hours after the yard had closed, and both Cranleigh and Guildford Brigades were called, but as our village possessed no mains water supply, after our own well, and those nearby, had been pumped dry, they were rendered helpless.

Everything had gone, he continued to tell me ; the fittings, machine, carpenter's and blacksmith's shops, together with the engine shed, office and stores. He pulled a handkerchief from his pocket and wiped his face, " All we have worked for, Jack, has gone," he murmured, swallowing the obvious lump in his throat. I sat down beside him staring into space, too numbed to speak . . . .

With all other records destroyed in the office were the maker's numbers of our road locomotive, tractions, tractors, steam wagons and portable engines, together with photographs of some of them when delivered to us new.

Although we were left with all our engines, sawmilling plants, and the latest addition to the firm, a three ton A.E.C. lorry, the loss of all the other equipment dealt us a staggering blow. Bravely Cyril struggled to re-build from the ashes, but a year or so later the strain became too heavy for him to bear and ill health forced him to give in. My mother and sister begged of me to carry on in Cyril's stead and, although I had the heart-felt backing of the whole of our staff, I knew that I could never, never, take the place of Cyril. Regretfully the decision was taken to sell the business. Three years after it had been sold there remained no sign of " steam " in any shape or form. Today where once stood a yard full of steam engines of all kinds, employing a whole village to work them, there is now, alas, no trace.

21

Epilogue:

The wagon rolls westward

again thirty-five years later

HAD ANYONE told me that I would again drive a steam wagon after thirty-five years away from them, also that my wife would be the owner of it, laughing until I cried would have been the greatest understatement of all times. For anyone more unlikely to own a steam wagon than my wife, and an " old timer " like me to drive it, even the Devil himself could not have conjured up. And, what is more, I would have given the teller a shilling to have his brains tested, and hydraulically at that.

Hot oil, steam and coal smoke is like a chronic disease; once you get a smell of it, you are its slave forever. When called upon to help a friend renovate an old traction engine to put in the Royal Counties Show at Horsham, Sussex, a few years ago, the bite that I received from a " Steam Bug " in my childhood flared up again good and proper.

Three years had passed from the Horsham Show when I heard of a steam wagon lying in a scrap yard at Ely. At this news the steam bug danced through my veins in an ecstasy of delight. Vainly I argued against buying it but the steam bug won, and once again after thirty-five years I became the owner of a Foden Steam Wagon.

After its delivery to my home by low-loader, my heart sank to the soles of my shoes, for a more dilapidated looking outfit one would be hard put-to to find. The " rust moths " appeared to have eaten most of it. The chimney, smokebox, side motion plates, coal bunker, footplate, water tank and various other bits were completely eaten away ; and many generations of woodworm had made their homes in the cab and other wood work. I cursed the steam bug to all eternity, but later upon close examination, after the removal of the grime of years, its " innards " were found to be in very good order.

The Log Book disclosed that she was built in 1930 and was delivered to the Northamptonshire County Council in June of that year ; classified as a " C " type, three-way Hydraulic Tipping, 6 ton wagon, Makers No. 13716.

Three years' hard labour of love passed in her rehabilitation, costing £200 or more, but at last the great day came when steam was raised for the first time. She looked lovely—her paint and bright work gleaming like the proverbial brass button.

My wife could not see eye to eye with me in the restoration of an old steam engine, but by a little cunning ingenuity on my part, she was persuaded to be present at the first trial run, and, she too got bitten by the steam bug. " I've heard you speak of an engine rally in Cornwall," said she, " Oh, do let's take her there. We can make a holiday of it." So, with a four-berth caravan behind giving ample accommodation for us both, and a friend acting as fireman, we set off for Redruth, Cornwall, 252 miles away, allowing ourselves four days to do it, in easy stages.

The day before setting off the water tank was filled ; oil, grease, gland packing and tools were put on board, together with 13 cwts. of coal (assuming we would be able to do 25 miles to the cwt. we should have a cwt. or so in hand). Normally this assumption would have been about right, but on this occasion things were far from normal.

The next morning steam was raised, and we were away, leaving our headquarters at Billingshurst, Sussex, at 10 a.m. The first stop was to be Havant, thirty miles away, where we were to pick up the caravan and my wife who had travelled from our head-quarters the day before to victual the caravan for our journey.

The first sign of trouble came within a few miles of our starting point. A decided shudder came with each revolution of the off-side rear wheel, and upon examination it was discovered that there was quite a marked " flat " in the twin solid rubber tyres. As the trouble did not appear to get worse, we decided to continue the journey.

Climbing Bury Hill brought home the fact that it was extremely difficult to keep a full head of steam, and unless the pressure was kept at 200-225 lbs. per square inch the engine had no power. All these things, of course, had not revealed themselves in previous short trial runs. The steaming trouble was due to the wrong size orifice in the exhaust blast pipe. This pipe had been eaten away by rust and Foden's could not help me in the matter as all their drawings had been destroyed long since. The answer could only be found by trial and error.

Havant was eventually reached and there it was discovered that one of the off-side mudguard stays had broken, due to the vibration caused by the flat in the tyres. The stay was welded up, the water tank filled, the caravan coupled up, then all three of us climbed aboard and we continued to roll westward.

Our next watering place was Romsey, but somehow we over shot the water-hole by about a mile. Our water tank being almost empty there was nothing for it but to uncouple the van, turn the wagon and go back in search of the water. Finding it this time and filling up, we returned to the van, coupled it on and resumed our journey, travelling on until we found a suitable lay-by where we pulled in and parked for the night. Distance covered on the first day's run —59 miles.

6.30 the next morning found us up and about, and while steam was being raised breakfast was served. By 8 a.m. we were rolling west again.

Salisbury was our next stop for water. Here the coal situation was reviewed, calculations were made, and it was discovered that we were falling far short of the 25 miles to the cwt., owing to the blast pipe already referred to. It was estimated that another 40 miles would bring us to the point of no return. Since steam coal is not readily obtained these days, we had to decide whether to go on or go back. My wife voted " go on," so go on it was.

The trouble of keeping steam grew gradually worse, and upon reaching Dinton, where I knew the village smith, I decided to try making some modifications to the blast pipe. I was given full use of the smithy, and a ferrule was made and fixed into position, giving far better results. While all this was being done, my wife cooked the lunch and in the general melee forgot to fasten the calor gas door of the caravan. After travelling for several minutes she remembered it and had to walk back half a mile to retrieve the door.

On then to Teffont Magna, through Mere to Ilchester, our next watering place. Here it was found that the off-side mud guard had again almost broken adrift and had been dancing a jig on the rear wheel, and in so doing had cut quite a heavy groove in one of the rubber tyres, so it was removed altogether and tossed on to the back of the wagon. As evening drew on the sky looked very ominous, and soon came a deluge of rain that at times made it difficult to see the road. Five miles west of Ilchester we found a lay-by and pulled in for the night. The distance run on the second day was 76 miles.

The next morning under a clear sky, we made an early start, reviewing the coal situation with growing apprehension. Water was taken on at Ilminster, but at our next proposed stop—Fenny Bridges, it was found to be out of reach of our suction hose, and we were unable to fill the tank. A dash had then to be made for Clyst Honiton, where we arrived with our tank completely empty and the water in the boiler just bobbing in the bottom of the gauge glass. Here I remembered the name of a coal merchant in Exeter who carried a stock of Welsh steam coal, and arranged with him, over the telephone, to meet us on the Exeter by-pass with 5 cwts. After our rendezvous with him we plodded on, taking on water ot the White Horse Garage, west of Exeter. Up hill, down hill, on and on picking up water at Sticklepath, Bridestowe, and Launceston. Reaching the edge of Bodmin Moor, about 7 p.m., half a mile beyond the Jamaica Inn, we found a place to pull off the road and bedded down for the night, but not before walking back to the Jamaica Inn for a " corpse reviver " to celebrate the day's run of 81 miles. The ferrule fitted at Dinton was doing fine work and we were taking most hills in top gear whereas hitherto we were changing gear at practically every incline.

The following morning found us on the road at 8 a.m. taking on water at the China Clay Works on the Moor. Then on through Bodmin and Indian Queeens, reaching the Mount Hawke (near Redruth) Rally ground at 11 a.m. Travelling distance on the fourth day 31 miles. We had used all told 18 cwts. of coal, and approximately 2,500 gallons of water.

The rally was a huge success, some 40 engines of all sorts attending, and there was an enormous crowd of interested people present. My wife was astir early on the rally morning cleaning brass and paint work. She was so thrilled with the wagon and all to do with it that I hadn't the heart to do anything else but make it her birthday present, a fact announced over the loud speakers.

During the evening after the rally a ton of coal was loaded up for the return journey. The only thing that marred a really wonderful day was a telegram from home requesting my wife to return on the coming Wednesday. We had intended to stay in Redruth for two or three days, but the news from home necessitated our leaving on the Sunday morning following the rally.

That evening instead of sight-seeing with our friends, the time was spent in preparing the wagon for the homeward run ; fire-grate cleaned out, tubes swept, lubricators filled, and all grease nipples charged with grease. At 9.30 a.m. on the following day we pulled out of the rally ground and headed for Okehampton to spend the night in a pull-off there. At 6.30 the next morning we were on the road again making for Exeter. About a mile from the city we stopped to fill up with water. As this was being done my wife, in the caravan, packed her bag in readiness to leave us, then almost in tears climbed into a friend's car to be speedily driven home, leaving my fireman and me to go on alone with the Foden wagon.

By evening we had reached Zeals and found a suitable place to pull off the road for the night, finishing the day's run early to enable us to repack the h.p. slide valve gland that had steadily grown worse during the afternoon in its blowing by of steam.

Leaving Zeals at 7.30 in the morning with the engine running perfectly we simply purred along, taking everything we came to in the way of hills in top gear, and reaching Havant, where we were to leave the caravan, just after 1.30 p.m. The caravan was cleaned out, and a hasty meal eaten, after which we were away again on the last lap of our journey back to headquarters. We finally reached Billingshurst at 6 p.m., breaking our own record for mileage in one day, by doing 102 miles.

The coal consumed on the return trip amounted to 16 cwts. Since this memorable Cornish journey, two new solid rubber tyres have been pressed on to the off-side rear wheel, and broken mud guard stays are now a thing of the past.

In the " old days " way back in the twenties, it would have been just another day's work. But now, as an " old timer," and having modern fast traffic to contend with, it has become more difficult. One gets a little more tired too with the passing years, but the love of steam lives on—the number of times we were photographed on the journey would prove that . . .

THE   END